CHILDREN'S BIBLE QUIZZING MINISTRY (CBQM)

Teacher's / Coach's Guide - Acts

Bible Study Lessons

Bible Quizzing

- Method using Games and Activities
- Method using Questions and Answers

> They devoted themselves to the apostles' teaching and to fellowship, to the breaking of bread and to prayer.
> Acts 2:42 (NIV)

Children's Bible Quizzing Ministry: Coach's Guide - Acts

Published by: Discipleship Ministries of the Mesoamerica Region

www.discipleship.MesoamericaRegion.org

www.SdmiResources.MesoamericaRegion.org

Copyright © 2019 - All rights reserved

ISBN: 978-1-63580-110-1

The people who participated in the original idea and production of the games and activities portion of this book are:
Carolina Ambrosio
Eva Velazquez
Patricia Picavea
Patricia Zamora

Adapted by: Pamela Vargas Castillo, with love for the children of the Church of the Nazarene

Printed in the United States

Welcome to the marvelous ministry of Children's Bible Quizzing

In this book you will find:

1. Lessons and questions

2. Guide for leading Children's Bible Quizzing using games and activities.

3. Guide for leading Children's Bible Quizzing using questions and answers (p. 125)

NOTE: It's important that you work with only one type of quizzing for competitions.

CONTENTS

Welcome!

Welcome to Bible Studies for Children: Acts! In this collection of biblical studies, children ages 6-12 years of age will learn about how Jesus' disciples spread God's love to the whole world!

This resource invites children to experience genuine discipleship through the study of God's transforming Word. They will learn about God, study his Word, and gain a saving knowledge of Jesus Christ. Children also learn to apply biblical teachings to actual life situations. These studies will encourage children to grow in Christlikeness and to live in relationship with God.

Our goals are to help your children:

- To desire to study the Bible
- To learn and develop Bible study habits
- To become familiar with God's holy Word
- To understand that God is the central character and hero of the Bible
- To understand the Bible as the story of God's redeeming love
- To begin a personal relationship with God through Jesus Christ
- To grow in wisdom, understanding, and Christlikeness
- To apply scripture to real life situations and reflect Christian attitudes.

The Book of Acts was written by a doctor named Luke who travelled with Paul on his journeys. The Book of Acts tells about Jesus' resurrection and ascension, the gift of the Holy Spirit and the beginning of the Church. It even tells when and where the word "Christian" was first used. Acts tells us how Christians today can continue to spread the good news about God's love.

Bible Studies for Children: Acts is one of six books in the cycle of the Bible Studies for Children series. These studies help children to gain an understanding of biblical chronology and the meaning of biblical events. As the children learn about the lives of the people in these studies, they discover God's love for all people and their place in his plan. God sometimes uses miracles to achieve his purpose. He often works through people to accomplish what he wants to do.

The philosophy of Bible Studies for Children is to help the children understand what the Bible says, learn how God helped the people, and grow in their relationship with God. This includes biblical study, biblical memorization, and application of biblical teachings in real life situations.

Bible Studies for Children uses the New International Version of the Bible.

BOOKS

The following is a short description of the books in this series and the way that they interact with each other.

Genesis provides the foundation. This book tells how God created the world from nothing, formed a man and a woman, and created a beautiful garden for their home. These people sinned, and they experienced the consequences for their sin. Genesis introduces the plan of God to reconcile the broken relationship between God and the people. It introduces Adam, Eve, Noah, Abraham, Isaac, and Jacob.

God made a covenant with Abraham and renewed that covenant with Isaac and Jacob. Genesis ends with the story of Joseph who saves civilization from famine. The famine compels the people of God to move to Egypt.

Exodus tells how God continued to keep his promise to Abraham. God rescued the Israelites from slavery in Egypt. The Lord chose Moses to guide the Israelites. The Lord set up his kingship over the Israelites. He led and ruled the Israelites through the establishment of the priesthood and the Tabernacle, the Ten Commandments and other laws, and the prophets and the judges. At the end of Exodus, only a part of the covenant of the Lord with Abraham is complete.

Joshua/Judges/Ruth tells how God completed his covenant with Abraham that began in Genesis. The Israelites conquered and settled into the land that God promised to Abraham.

The prophets, the priests, the Law, and the worship rituals declared that God was the Lord and the King of the Israelites. The 12 tribes of Israel settled into the Promised Land. This study emphasizes these judges: Deborah, Gideon, and Samson.

In **1 and 2 Samuel**, the Israelites wanted a king because the other nations had a king. These books tell about Samuel, Saul, and David. Jerusalem became the center of the combined nation of Israel. This study shows how the people reacted differently when someone confronted them with their sins. While Saul blamed others or made excuses, David admitted his sin, and he asked God for forgiveness.

Matthew is the focal point of the entire series. It focuses on the birth, the life, and the ministry of Jesus. All the previous books in the series pointed to Jesus as the Son of God and the Messiah. Jesus ushered in a new era. The children learn about this new era in several events: the teachings of Jesus, his death, his resurrection, and the mentoring of his disciples. Through Jesus, God provided a new way for the people to have a relationship with him.

At the beginning of **Acts**, Jesus ascended to heaven, and God sent the Holy Spirit to help the Church. The good news of salvation through Jesus Christ spread to many parts of the world. The believers preached the gospel to the Gentiles, and missionary work began. The message of the love of God transformed both the Jews and the Gentiles. There is a direct connection between the evangelism efforts of Paul and Peter to the lives of the people today.

CYCLE

The following cycle of this series is specifically for those who participate in the optional Bible Quizzing aspect of Bible Studies for Children.

You will find more information about this in the section called "Children's Bible Quizzing" (page 143).

- Acts (2018-2019)
- Genesis (2019-2020)
- Exodus (2020-2021)
- Joshua, Judges and Ruth (2021-2022)
- 1 & 2 Samuel (2022-2023)
- Matthew (2023-2024)

SCHEDULE

Each book of the series has about 20 lessons. Each lesson is designed for 1 to 2 hours for class time. The following Schedule is one suggestion for each study:

- 15 minutes for the Activity
- 30 minutes for the Bible Lesson
- 15 minutes for the Memory Verse
- 30 minutes for Additional Activities (optional)
- 30 minutes for practicing the Bible Quizzing (optional)

PREPARATION FOR THE TEACHER

Thorough preparation of each study is important. The children are more attentive and gain better understanding of the study if you prepare it well and present it well. The following steps will help you prepare.

Step 1: Quick Overview. Read the Key Verse and Teaching Objectives.

Paso 2: Bible Passage and Bible Commentary. Read the verses of the Biblical Passage for the lesson and the information of the Biblical Commentary, as well as the Words related to our Faith, People, Places, and Objects that are included.

Step 3: Opening Activity. This section includes a game or other activity with the goal of preparing the children for the Bible lesson. Familiarize yourself with the activity, the instructions, and the materials. Take the materials that you'll need to class. Prepare the activity before the children arrive.

Step 4: Bible Lesson. Review the lesson and learn it so that you tell it as a story. The children want the teacher to tell the story rather than to read it from the book.

Use the Words of Our Faith from each lesson to provide additional information as you tell the story. After the story, use the review questions. They will help the children to understand the story and to apply it to their lives.

Paso 5: Memory Verse (Key Verse).

Learn the memory verse before you teach it to the children. On page 61, there are suggestions for memorization. Choose from the activities to help the children to learn the memory verse. Become familiar with the activity that you choose. Read the instructions and prepare the supplies that you will bring to class.

Step 6: Suggested Activities.

The Suggested Activities reinforce the Children's Bible Study using games and activities (included in this book). Many of these activities require additional supplies, resources, and time.

Become familiar with the activities that you choose. Read the instructions and prepare the supplies that you will bring to class.

Step 7: Review the questions about the study

Step 8 (Optional): Practice for the Bible Quizzing Competition using the method of questions and answers. This is a type of competition of Bible Studies for children. More information can be found in the section titled, "Guide for Bible Quizzing using Questions and Answers" (p. 125). If you decide to participate in this type of quizzing, spend time with the children in preparation. There are practice questions for each study. The first 10 questions are for the basic level of competition. The following 10 questions are for the advanced level of competition. With the guidance of the teacher, the children choose their level of competition.

THE PROMISED GIFT
Lesson 1

BIBLICAL PASSAGE: Acts 1:1-2:47

KEY VERSE: *But you will receive power when the Holy Spirit comes on you; and you will be my witnesses in Jerusalem, and in all Judea and Samaria, and to the ends of the earth.* (Acts 1:8).

TEACHING OBJECTIVES - To help the children:

1. Know the Holy Spirit as guide of our lives and to recognize his guidance in spreading the gospel.
2. Know that the Holy Spirit is God's gift for us.

BIBLICAL COMMENTARY

Luke's book, Acts of the Apostles, invites readers to continue the mission of Christ until his return. For forty days, Jesus prepared his followers to continue his mission. "Forty" reminds us of those who were tested before they began their ministries: The Israelites as they wandered in the desert, Moses on Mt. Sinai, Elijah as he fled to Horeb.

Jesus echoes the prophecy of Isaiah 32:15. It is the Spirit who enables believers to effectively witness to the entire world.

Jesus' followers were baptized with the Holy Spirit on Pentecost. Originally, Pentecost (also known as the Feast of Weeks) celebrated God's gift of the Ten Commandments to Moses and the people of Israel, fifty days after the Exodus from Egypt. For Christians today, Pentecost is a celebration of God's gift of his Spirit to all believers, fifty days after Easter Sunday.

God poured out his Spirit on the community of believers. The Spirit unified them and gave them a passion to follow Christ. They received the power to intelligibly communicate the truth of Jesus to the entire world.

Peter invited his listeners to repent and be baptized. New believers joined the community of faith, and they grew in their faith by obeying the apostles' teaching, praying daily, and sharing with those in need. In these first two chapters, we see the start of Jesus' mission to bring freedom from sin, and see that message spread to the ends of the earth.

The Early Church had hope. They saw that God continued to transform them by the power of the Holy Spirit. God was revealing his kingdom on earth. They were excited to share this good news with everyone. As believers, we continue the mission started by the faithful Church over two thousand years ago. Likewise, we can experience the power of the Holy Spirit, and, we will be witnesses of God's kingdom when God changes us.

WORDS OF OUR FAITH

The Holy Spirit — the Spirit of God. The Holy Spirit empowers us to live for God as we trust Jesus as Savior.

Jesus Christ — Jesus is God's son, the Savior of the world. Jesus is fully God and fully human. Christ is a Greek word that means "the anointed one."

The Messiah — Messiah is a Hebrew word that means "the anointed one" and is usually translated as "the Christ." It refers to Jesus Christ.

Peter — one of Jesus' 12 disciples. He preached the first sermon at Pentecost and was a leader in the Early Church.

Jerusalem — the center of the Jewish religion. Jerusalem is the geographical focal point for much of the Bible.

Pentecost — a Jewish religious festival held 50 days after Passover. Christians celebrate this as the day the Holy Spirit came and the Early Church was born.

The Apostles — early leaders of the Christian Church who were specially chosen by Jesus. They were God's ambassadors as the Church grew and spread.

Baptism — a public ceremony that symbolizes a person's rebirth in Jesus Christ. Baptism is a ritual in which a believer is immersed in water or has water sprinkled or poured on his or her head. A believer chooses to be baptized to show that they are beginning a new life in Christ.

The Jews — people who practice the Jewish religion. God established a covenant with Abraham in Genesis 15 and 17. The Jews are known as the descendants of Abraham and his son and grandson

(Isaac and Jacob). The Bible also calls them Israelites.

Prophesy — a message from God to people. Some prophecies tell what will happen in the future.

OPENING ACTIVITY

Party time! You can decorate your classroom or place where you meet as if to celebrate a birthday party. You can even bring a cake. If it's not possible to have a party, start your session by asking your children to describe in detail the "perfect party".

Let the group share their ideas for a while, and when you are ready to start the Bible study, give them the following two questions in writing or simply read them out loud and ask the group to answer.

The first question has to do with the definition of the word church. Obviously we use it for many things, as the response options indicate. The correct answer is not printed: "All the previous ones". All the answers are correct, depending on the desired meaning. Take a moment to help your class focus on the last answer, "all the Christians of the world." That is the definition of "church" that we will use today.

The second question is more difficult. The correct answer is: "The day that the Holy Spirit filled the apostles (Pentecost)." Use this as a transition to the lesson.

What is the definition of the word "church"? Choose one of the following answers:

    a. A building where people worship
    b. The people who worship in that building
    c. The time these people gather to worship
    d. All the people in a certain denomination.
    e. All the Christians of the world.

If you had to choose a day to celebrate the birthday of the Church, which of these would you choose?
    1. The day Jesus was born (Christmas)
    2. The day Jesus was crucified (Good Friday)
    3. The day Jesus rose from the dead (Easter)
    4. The day that Jesus returned to heaven
    5. The day the Holy Spirit filled the apostles (Pentecost)

BIBLE LESSON

1. Good-bye ... for now (1:1-11)

Acts is the second volume of a set of two books that began with the book of Luke. In volume one, Luke wrote "everything that Jesus began to do and teach" (Acts 1:1). Now he is going to talk about the things that Jesus continued to do, through His Church.

Luke begins his story with a brief summary of the last chapter of volume one (see Luke 24), which describes several of Jesus' appearances after His crucifixion and resurrection. Then he describes Jesus' ascension to heaven.

* Ask the children to place on the map the three specific areas where the gospel was to be spread (1: 8).

2. And the winner is... (1:12-26)

After Jesus' ascension, Peter, who was obviously the leader of the group of Christians, felt the need to replace Judas to keep the number of apostles at 12. The criteria for choosing the twelfth apostle, which Peter quotes in verses 21-23, was that it was someone who had been part of the earthly ministry of Jesus from the beginning and who was a witness of the Resurrection. Two men met those requirements: Joseph called Barsabbas and Matthias. After praying, the apostles cast lots and selected Matthias.

Who were these men? We don't know. But the apostles prayed about the matter and drew lots. And so they chose Matthias.

3. The birthday of the Church (2:1-41)

In this chapter, Luke records the events of the day considered as the birthday of the Church, the Day of Pentecost.

Pentecost was one of the main Jewish festivities. It takes place on the 50th day after Easter, and gets its name from the Greek word meaning "50". On that day, the Christians "were all together in the same place" (2:1). No doubt you already know what happened next. First the sound of a violent wind came from the sky (v. 2).

Then tongues like fire appeared on the head of each of the Christians (verse 3). And then, when they were individually and collectively filled with the Holy Spirit, they began to speak in "different tongues" (v. 4).

It is important to note that these "other languages" were not incomprehensible languages but rather known languages, the languages of the pilgrims that were in Jerusalem that day (see v. 8-11).

* Draw the miraculous signs that accompanied the moment when the believers were filled with the Holy Spirit.

Then Peter stood up and gave the first Christian sermon of the truth of the gospel.

* Ask the children to read Peter's sermon and summarize it in two or three sentences. (2:15-36)

4. The daily life of the Church (2:42-47)

This short passage allows us to see the daily lives of Christians during the first weeks of the Church.

* Make a list of the activities that believers did every day (2:42-47).

Is there a word that appears frequently on this list? Of course, together. The Early Church understood the importance of being close to one another. That must have been an exciting time!

SUGGESTED ACTIVITIES

* Ask the children to start making a glossary at home of the Words of our Faith.

* Make a list with the name of the characters, places and objects that appear in this passage to be added to the glossary.

* Do the games in this book that are related to this lesson: crossword puzzle, finish the story, and games of the arts and crafts category.

QUESTIONS

1. To whom is the book of Acts written? (1:1)
Theophilus

2. Why did Jesus command the disciples not to leave Jerusalem? (1:4-5)
They were to wait there for the Father's promise of the Holy Spirit.

3. Where would the apostles be witnesses once they had received the Holy Spirit? (1:8)
Jerusalem, Judea, Samaria and to the ends of the earth.

4. According to Acts 1:15, how many people were in the group of believers in those days?
120

5. Who was chosen by lot to replace Judas? (1:26)
Matthias

6. What are the three signs that occurred at Pentecost? (2:2-4)
* A violent gust of wind
* Tongues of fire
* They spoke different languages.

7. Who will be saved? (2:21)
Everyone who calls on the name of the Lord.

8. According to Acts 2:41, how many people joined the church?
About three thousand.

BETTER THAN MONEY

Lesson 2

BIBLICAL PASSAGE: Acts 3:1-4:31

KEY VERSE: *Salvation is found in no one else, for there is no other name under heaven given to mankind by which we must be saved.* (Acts 4:12).

TEACHING OBJECTIVES - To help the children:

1. Feel good about the gifts that God has given them.
2. Give glory to God for their gifts.
3. Know that the Holy Spirit gives us courage to testify about Jesus.

BIBLICAL COMMENTARY

As Peter and John approached the Temple for prayer, a beggar called out and asked them for money. Because of the beggar's physical condition, he was unable to worship God in the Temple. He was unclean, an outsider.

Instead of giving him money, Peter healed him in the name of Jesus. (See Luke 13:10-13 for a similar incident by Jesus, one of the many stories where Jesus healed people.) In this story we get a glimpse of what the book of Acts is about: the early believers shared the good news about Jesus and salvation with everyone, not just the religious insiders.

The beggar, fully restored, joined Peter and John in praising God. Peter declared that the healing of the beggar happened by the name of Jesus. We see that Jesus' power is not limited. He can do miraculous things in order to heal and save people.

The religious leaders arrested Peter and John. However, the apostles were prepared because Jesus taught them not to worry about what to say when this happens. The Holy Spirit would help them (Luke 12:11-12). So guided by the Holy Spirit, Peter spoke confidently in front of this group of angry, religious leaders. He repeated his message of good news about Jesus, who alone brings salvation.

The Sanhedrin didn't want this message about Jesus to spread. They commanded the apostles to stop preaching in the name of Jesus. Peter and John recognized that their first obligation was to obey God. The Spirit enabled Peter, the faithful witness, to speak courageously. Only months earlier, Peter had denied his association with Jesus. However, after Pentecost, he was able to publicly defend his Lord.

WORDS OF OUR FAITH

The Sadducees — Jewish leaders from families of priests who believed in strictly following the Law of Moses. They did not believe in the resurrection of the dead or in angels. (They were also called "teachers of the law.")

To repent — to turn away from the sin and to turn to God.

Clean & unclean — categories that define certain people, animals and food according to Jewish law and customs. Usually, someone could make an unclean thing clean by preforming a special ritual, called a ceremonial washing. In the New Testament, Jesus demonstrated that clean and unclean was more internal than external. Only God can make a person clean. See Ezekiel 36:24-27 for more information.

Salvation — everything that God does to forgive people of their sins and to help them obey him. Only God can save people from sin.

The Sanhedrin — a group of Jewish leaders who acted as a legal court.

A witness — someone who tells others what he or she saw or experienced. A Christian witness is a person who tells others about Jesus and salvation.

A temple — a special place of worship in Jerusalem used by the Jews in biblical times. The first temple was built by Solomon. See 1 Kings 6 for details.

OPENING ACTIVITY

For this activity you will need the following:

• Masking tape, optional (you can choose another way to designate "jail" in the lesson)

Before class, use tape to designate a large square space on the floor to make a "jail." This area should be large enough for the children to stop or sit there.

During the study, read and discuss the main points of the Bible story. Lead the dialogue so that the children talk about Jesus. Every time someone mentions Jesus, he or she must go to jail. Say: *In the time of Peter and John, many believers were arrested and locked up in jail for talking about Jesus. What do they think they were doing in prison?*

BIBLE LESSON

1. Is there something better than gold or silver? (3:1-10)

Without medical help, disabled people in ancient Israel who did not come from wealthy families had only one option: begging for survival. This passage tells the story of such a person, a man about 40 years old (see 4:22), who had been crippled since he was born.

One day, Peter and John went to the Temple to pray. See how they kept the traditions of the Jewish religion. The early Christians continued to be faithful Hebrews, with no intention of breaking with their religion of birth. They saw Christianity as the fulfillment, not as a replacement, of Judaism.

At the door of the Temple, the apostles found this disabled person with his daily custom of asking for alms to satisfy his basic needs.

* After reading this short passage, ask the children and let them respond:

1. When Peter said, "Silver or gold I do not have" (v. 6), what do you think he meant? Choose one of the answers:
  * "We are poor like you."
  * "We forgot the money at home."
  * "We believe that it is not money that you need."
  * "Compared to what we have to give you, money is nothing."

2. Did Peter accept the credit for healing the man? (v. 6)

3. What did the man do after he was healed? (v. 8)

4. What was the response of the people in the Temple when they saw the man? (v. 10)

2. Peter preached his second sermon (3:11-26)

Seeing this man, who had been begging at the door of the Temple for years, running and jumping made people gather. And Peter, like many preachers, took advantage of the situation. This was a golden opportunity to preach another sermon.

* Help the children read the sermon recorded in these verses and then compare it to the sermon in 2:14-41.

How are they similar? How are they different?

3. Good sermon, Peter. We caught you. (4:1-22)

Just as Peter was about to finish his sermon and make an invitation, he was interrupted by the Temple guards and the Jewish officers. They were not very happy about all the fuss, especially when they realized that Peter was preaching again about Jesus. So they put him in jail for one night.

The next day Peter was brought before the Council (Sanhedrin), the supreme Jewish court.

4. The response of the congregation (4:23-31)

After Peter and John were released, they returned to their Christian community, where they had a prayer meeting. (Notice that wonderful word "together" in verse 24). This prayer reveals how the first Christians responded to the persecution that day, and how they intended to respond in the future.

In verse 29, the apostles have a battle plan. How did God respond to their prayer? (V. 31)

SUGGESTED ACTIVITIES

  • Continue with the glossary of Words of our Faith.
  • Add to the list, the characters, places and objects that appear in this lesson.
  • Do the games that are related to this lesson: How do you imagine it?, Flags.

QUESTIONS

Acts 3-4:22

1. Where was a man crippled from birth? (3:2)
Next to the gate called Beautiful.

2. Of what is Jesus the author? (3:15)
Life

3. What gave complete health to the man crippled at birth? (3:16)
Faith in the name of Jesus.

4. Where did Peter and John go until the next day? (4:3)
Jail

5. How many men believed, after hearing Peter's sermon at Solomon's Colonnade? (4:4)
About five thousand

6. What did the religious leaders command Peter and John to do? (4:18)
Stop talking and teaching in the name of Jesus.

7. What did the believers ask God in prayer to do for them after Peter and John's release from jail? (4:29)
Consider their threats and enable your servants to speak your word with great boldness.

8. What happened after they prayed that prayer? (Acts 4:31)
The place where they were meeting was shaken. And they were all filled with the Holy Spirit and spoke the word of God boldly.

ONE IN HEART & MIND
Lesson 3

BIBLICAL PASSAGE: Acts 4:32-5:42

KEY VERSE: *All the believers were one in heart and mind. No one claimed that any of their possessions was their own, but they shared everything they had.* (Acts 4:32).

TEACHING OBJECTIVES - To help the children:

1. Desire lives of real obedience.
2. Know that God supplies our needs through obedient people.

BIBLICAL COMMENTARY

The believers of the Early Church sometimes chose to share their property, or the money from the sale of their property, with others. Charity among the community encouraged friendship, maturity, and a radical trust in God. However, giving money and property was voluntary.

There are two different examples of believers who shared their possessions: one through honesty and one through deceit.

Barnabas sold a field and gave the money to the apostles. This is an example of a faithful and honest giver. Later, we will learn about Barnabas' role as an encourager to the believers when he supported Paul in ministry.

In contrast to Barnabas were two other believers: Ananias and his wife Sapphira. They also sold their property, but they kept some of the money for themselves. When they gave part of the money to the disciples, they pretended that it was the full amount. In this story, we have the first record of sin in the Early Church. They sinned by lying to God and others.

The apostles gave both of them the opportunity to repent, but they continued to lie. Their punishment was quick, and they both died.

Ananias and Sapphira's punishment may seem harsh. However, the Early Church learned an important lesson. Even though their faith in Jesus freed them from some of the restrictions of the Jewish laws, it did not mean that they were free to be immoral. Lying and disrespect for authority had no place in the community of faith.

Unfortunately, the Spirit's work in Ananias and Sapphira's lives didn't change their love of prestige and money. However, the Spirit's work in the lives of believers should lead to freedom and generosity, as exemplified by Barnabas. Let's follow his example!

WORDS OF OUR FAITH

Believer — The person who believes that Jesus is the Son of God. The believers accepted Jesus as their Savior, loved him and obeyed him.

OPENING ACTIVITY

For this activity you will need the following:

- A cheap gift for each student (for example: a piece of fruit, bread, cookie, candy, a toy or something simple)
- Toy money (use money from a game or make your own, cutting strips of paper and writing different amounts on each) Distribute cheap gifts to some of the children, not all.

Tell them not to play with their new possession or eat them. Designate an adult leader or child to take care of the toy money. Encourage the children to sell their possessions and then give the money to someone who does not have a possession. Encourage the banker to buy and sell things so that, in the end, each student has a gift.

Say: *Gifts represent our daily needs. God wants us to be compassionate and generous to one another. When we give, we help those in need. The first Christians helped others and we can also do it.*

Discuss how the first Christians helped one another by selling some of their possessions to help those in need.

BIBLE LESSON

1. Share and share equally (4:32-37)

This passage begins with a wonderful statement: "All the believers were one in heart and mind." Sadly, that claim has rarely been true in the 2 thousand years that have passed since then.

The harmony and unity among those early Christians was so complete that it extended into their pockets. Each believer contributed his

15

personal finances to a common treasury, from which money was distributed according to the need. So effective was this system that "there were no needy persons among them" (v. 34).

2. Problems from within (5:1-11)

It was not enough that the apostles had problems from the outside; they soon began having them from within the Christian community as well.

In the previous passage, we read of the distribution of wealth and goods among Christians in Jerusalem. The last verses we read (4:36-37) give us the example of Joseph the Levite (also called Barnabas). Now we find Ananias and Sapphira who also sold land and donated it to the community.

But something went wrong between the sale and the donation.

* Ask the children to read the passage and then ask them:

1. The money that Ananias and Sapphira gave to the apostles was certainly a generous donation. What was wrong with it?

2. What was the true sin of the couple? (v. 4)

3. Why do you think God gave them such a harsh punishment?

3. The fame of the community spread (5:12-16)

As we read in 2:43, the apostles continued to perform "many wonders and signs." This was a time of global importance. The outpouring of the Holy Spirit on humanity, which began on the Day of Pentecost, was powerful and spectacular.

The news of these signs and wonders filled Jerusalem and the neighboring towns. They brought multitudes of sick people to the disciples to be healed. Even so, when the believers met in a public space, like Solomon's Colonnade, "no one else dared join them" (v. 13).

4. Problems from outside (5:17-42)

As you will recall from chapter 4, when Peter and John were arrested the first time, the Jewish leaders "commanded them not to speak or teach at all in the name of Jesus" (4:18). Obviously, the apostles didn't obey the order.

Therefore, it is no surprise that the Christian leaders were put in jail once again. However, this time they didn't stay there for long. An angel came at midnight and took them out, and at dawn they were back in the temple courts preaching and teaching again. Despite the scourging, the apostles left the Council "full of joy." Although most of us have never experienced severe punishment because of our faith, our brothers and sisters in Christ in other parts of the world still suffer.

SUGGESTED ACTIVITIES

- Continue with the glossary of Words of our Faith.
- Add to the list the characters, places and objects that appear in this lesson.
- Do the games that are related to this lesson: Finish the story, Modern Day Bible, Charades, Breaking News, and games of the Arts and Crafts category.

QUESTIONS
CHAPTERS 4-5

1. Who were one in heart and mind? (4:32)
All the believers.

2. What nickname did the apostles give Joseph the Levite from Cyprus? (4:36)
Barnabas, which means encouragement.

3. What did Joseph, also called Barnabas, do with the money from the land he sold? (4:37)
He put it at the feet of the apostles.

4. According to Acts 5:4, who did Ananias lie?
Not just to human beings, but to God.

5. Who died for having lied to God? (5:1-11)
Ananias and Sapphira.

6. What took hold of the church and all who had heard about the death of Ananias and Sapphira? (5:11)
A great fear.

7. Where did they all meet by mutual agreement? (5:12)
Solomon's Colonnade.

8. Recite from memory Acts 5:29
"Peter and the other apostles replied: "We must obey God rather than human beings!"

THE CHURCH SPREADS

Lesson 4

BIBLICAL PASSAGE: Acts 6:1-8:3

KEY VERSE: *So the Word of God spread. The number of disciples in Jerusalem increased rapidly, and a large number of priests became obedient to the faith.* (Acts 6:7)

TEACHING OBJECTIVES - To help the children:

1. Defend the right thing, even when they are alone.

2. Know that God always is with us. Even in times of persecution, we must depend on him to remain strong.

BIBLICAL COMMENTARY

The Early Church faced many problems, including prejudice and persecution. The first Christians were known for their generosity and charity. However, a problem of unfair food distribution threatened to divide the Church. The apostles handled the conflict well. They recognized the need for more leaders to work in specific areas of ministry.

Stephen was one of those leaders to whom the apostles gave administrative duties. The apostles chose him and six others. These men were wise and filled with the Holy Spirit. Because of their faithfulness, the good news about Jesus spread quickly.

Stephen's ministry was not limited to food distribution. He preached and performed miracles, like the ones prophesied by Joel and mentioned in Peter's sermon on the day of Pentecost. Like Peter, his preaching was not welcomed by some religious leaders. They lied, and hired other people to lie, so that Stephen would be brought to their religious court, the Sanhedrin, for a trial. Though Stephen was innocent, and his accusers were liars, the Sanhedrin executed him.

Stephen's life and death are similar to other biblical stories. Stephen's vision of God is an echo of the story of Moses' meeting with God on Mt. Sinai (Exodus 34:29).

The accusations made against Stephen are similar to those made against Jesus. Stephen compared his accusers to the unrepentant Israelites in the desert. Like Jesus, Stephen's concern at the time of his death was the forgiveness of his killers. Stephen became the first Christian martyr, and he reflected the heart and mind of Jesus in life as well as at his death.

After Stephen's execution, a period of persecution against the Church began. At the end of Stephen's story, the reader of Acts is introduced to Saul, a main character in the book.

Saul and other opponents of Christianity tried to eliminate the message of Jesus Christ by persecuting the early believers.

However, instead of hindering the message, this persecution scattered the believers and caused God's message to spread further. These believers trusted the Holy Spirit to help them each day to be bold and share God's message everywhere they went.

WORDS OF OUR FAITH

Blasphemy — the act of speaking inappropriately about God. People often accused Jesus of blasphemy.

A prophet— someone whom God has chosen to receive and deliver his messages.

A synagogue — The word means "assembly" and in the Bible it refers to a Jewish place of prayer.

Persecution— physical abuse, ridicule, or suffering a person experiences from others for what he or she believes.

Prejudice— a preconceived idea or bias toward members of a certain group.

Forgiveness — the act of releasing someone from a punishment that they deserve.

OPENING ACTIVITY

For this activity you will need the following:

• Phosphorescent or luminous wands (glow sticks), small lanterns or candles. During the study, give each student a glow stick, flashlight or candle. Ask the children to stand in line. Turn off all the lights and ask the first child to make a light (breaking the glow stick, lighting the lantern or candle). Then ask the next child to do the same. Continue with the row until you create a chain of lights.

Ask: What was the room like before you made light?

What happened as more people turned on their lights?

How does this illustrate what happens in the world as people hear the gospel?

Say: *Just as together we created a chain of lights, the disciples needed help to care for the believers and spread the light of the good news about Jesus. What did they do to get the help they needed?*

BIBLE LESSON

1. Your server for today will be... (6:1-7)

When we read 4:32-35, we see that the community in Jerusalem lived in a type of commune. The economic assets of the members went to a common fund and the money was distributed according to the needs of each one.

As the community grew, this system became complicated. The apostles, no doubt, had difficulty keeping up with the daily work of the distribution as well as their tasks of preaching, teaching and leading the group. (Especially since they were being arrested and put in jail on a regular basis.)

Although the community so far consisted entirely of Jews, there were two different groups represented. One group was that of the "Aramaic-speaking Jews"; that is, those who had lived in Israel all their lives. The other group were the "Greek Jews", the foreigners, and some of them had surely gone to Jerusalem to celebrate Pentecost and had converted to Christianity, and then stayed in Jerusalem to be part of the Christian community.

These Greek Jews began to feel that the distribution of goods, especially food, was not being equitable with the Aramaic-speaking Jews. They complained about favoritism.

This complaint caused the apostles to open a new job in the community.

* Ask the children to make a list of the requirements that were used to choose the people in charge of serving the tables.

2. The arrest of Stephen (6:8-15)

As soon as these seven men were appointed to take care of the daily administration of the community, the first of them, Stephen, was arrested. The privilege of being arrested was not limited only to the apostles. Lay people like Stephen were also at risk.

* Ask the children to read the passage and answer the following questions:

1. What does verse 8 tell us about Stephen?

2. What were the accusations against Stephen?

3. In the heat of the interrogation before the Council we can imagine how the tension went up. But what was Stephen's reaction to the trial? (v. 15)

3. That man knows how to preach! (7:1-53)

When Stephen was asked to answer the accusations against him, he not only replied ... he preached. This sermon is the longest in the book of Acts. Stephen had three main themes:

1. The heroes of the Jews were men who were not afraid to obey God's call, even if it meant packing and moving away from home.

2. The Jewish nation had worshiped God much earlier, when there was not even a temple.

3. When the Jewish leaders caused the crucifixion of Jesus, they were following a historical pattern of persecution and destruction of the prophets.

* Read Stephen's sermon slowly with the children, as it contains many important ideas. Then have them answer these questions:

1. In Stephen's account of Jewish history, he referred to many stories that were well known. Are there any in particular that you consider special?

2. Verse 48 says, "the Most High does not live in houses made by human hands." Write that idea in your own words.

The first martyr (7:54-8:3)

Stephen's listeners "were furious and gnashed their teeth" (verse 54). They were so angry with Stephen that, in fact, they dragged him out of the city and stoned him to death, making him the first Christian martyr to die for his faith.

The Bible tells us the story of a day in Stephen's life. One day and nothing more. But that day was the last of his life.

If today was the only day of your life that would be written in history, what would be written about you?

You noticed that there was a special witness to Stephen's death. Who was he? (v. 58)

SUGGESTED ACTIVITIES

● Continue with the glossary of Words of our Faith. Add to the list the characters, places and objects that appear in this lesson.

● Do the games that are related to this lesson: Help the Missionaries.

QUESTIONS

CHAPTERS 6-8:3

1. Who said, "It would not be right for us to neglect the ministry of the Word of God in order to wait on tables"? (6:1-2)
The twelve to the multitude of the disciples.

2. What men did they choose to serve at the tables? (6:5)
Stephen, Philip, Procorus, Nicanor, Timon, Parmenas, and Nicolas

3. Who was full of grace and power? (6: 8)
Stephen

4. According to Acts 6:13, what did the false witnesses testify?
This fellow never stops speaking against this holy place and against the law

5. What did Stephen see when he looked up to heaven? (7:55)
He saw the glory of God, and Jesus standing at the right hand of God.

6. What did Stephen say in his prayer while they were stoning him? (7:59)
Lord Jesus, receive my spirit.

7. When Stephen fell to his knees, what did he cry out? (7:60)
Lord, do not hold this sin against them.

8. Who was there approving Stephen's death? (8: 1)
Saul

9. Who buried Stephen? (8: 2)
Godly men

PHILLIP ON THE ROAD

Lesson 5

BIBLICAL PASSAGE: Acts 8:4-40

KEY VERSE: "Those who had been scattered preached the word wherever they went. Philip went down to a city in Samaria and proclaimed the Messiah there" (Acts 8:4-5).

TEACHING OBJECTIVES - To help the children:

1. Understand that God helps us understand his Word so we can have a relationship with him.

2. Share Christ with my friends.

BIBLICAL COMMENTARY

After the Church scattered, believers preached wherever they went.

Philip was one of the early believers who left Jerusalem because of the persecution. He went to Samaria and preached about the kingdom of God. Because of his obedience, many people believed and were baptized, including a sorcerer named Simon.

Because of Philip's faithful work, Peter and John came from Jerusalem to pray for the new believers. The apostles put their hands on them, and they received the Holy Spirit. When Simon saw this, he wanted to buy the ability to give the Holy Spirit to people. Like Ananias and Sapphira, we have a story of an early believer committing a sin, and the apostles quickly correcting the situation.

Peter rebuked Simon because he was more impressed with the display of power than the concern for other people's salvation. He wanted to control God's Spirit so that he could continue to be a powerful person. Peter said that Simon's heart was not right before God. Peter told him to repent of his wickedness. Simon recognized Peter's authority and asked him to pray for him. It is unclear whether Peter did this or not, or if Simon repented for his sin. Repentance involves a change

of thought, intentions, and actions: to turn away from selfish desires and to turn toward God.

Next, the Spirit led Philip to speak to an Ethiopian eunuch.

According to Deuteronomy 23:1, a eunuch was not allowed to enter the Temple. Even so, he was a devout man, and he went to Jerusalem to worship. He was on his way home when he met Philip. Philip explained to him that Jesus was the Christ. This news about Jesus helped the Ethiopian to better understand God's message of love. This revelation changed his life. Philip baptized the Ethiopian.

WORDS OF OUR FAITH

Magician or sorcerer — A person who practices black magic, or who uses enchantments or spells to obtain supernatural powers through evil spirits. Simon was a wizard or sorcerer who boasted of his power instead of the power of God.

Sin — To disobey God. To sin is to put one's will above the will of God. Sin can refer to the spiritual condition or action of a person.

Eunuch — A man who cannot have children. Eunuchs were often members of the royal court.

OPENING ACTIVITY

Before class, ask for the help of an adult who likes to do funny things that make children laugh. During class, encourage children to play "Follow the leader."

The leader will perform an action (jumping repeatedly, jumping on one foot, bending his ears, etc.). The children will imitate what the leader does. After a few seconds, the leader will change action and the students should do exactly the same. The duration of the game will depend on the time you have available.

Say: The Bible lesson today is about Philip. Saul sought Christians to arrest them. He went from house to house to find them. Since the Christians were no longer safe in Jerusalem, they went in different directions. When Philip left Jerusalem, he followed his leader: God. The Spirit of God guided him to Samaria and to the desert. In today's lesson we'll learn more about what Philip did when he followed his leader.

BIBLE LESSON

1. The gospel comes to Samaria (8:4-25)

Before you study this passage, go back and read 8:1-3 again. There we read that "On that day a great persecution broke out against the church in Jerusalem, and all except the apostles were scattered throughout Judea and Samaria."

One of the scattered Christians was Philip, the deacon we met in 6:5. He went to Samaria, a country north of Jerusalem, populated by people of Jewish origin but who had married pagans. The Jews hated them, and when they traveled, they used to go out of their way thousands of kilometers just to avoid going to Samaria.

* Ask the children to identify Samaria on the map.

Notice that the Holy Spirit had not yet been given in many places. What did Peter and John do in v. 15-17.

2. Evangelism face to face (8:26-40)

After the massive evangelization of Philip in Samaria, and angel of the Lord instructed him simply to "go." On the way, he met an Ethiopian, an African in charge of the official treasure in his country. Under the leadership of the Holy Spirit, Philip played a key role in the conversion of this man.

* Read this passage together with the children and then answer the following questions:

1. According to Luke, the angel told Philip to go, but he didn't tell him why. How do you feel about Philip's blind faith?

2. The Ethiopian was either a Jewish convert or a student of Judaism, because he had gone to Jerusalem to worship and was reading the book of Isaiah when Philip found him (verses 27-28). Do you think that the Lord had already prepared his heart to receive Philip's testimony?

3. In the passage, the Ethiopian is reading Isaiah 53. Take a few moments to read that chapter in the Old Testament. Sum it up in one or two sentences.

4. What do you think is most important ... mass evangelism, like what Philip did in Samaria (v. 4-8), or personal face to face, like what Philip did with the Ethiopian?

SUGGESTED ACTIVITIES

- Continue with the glossary of Words of our Faith.

- Add to the list the characters, places and objects that appear in this lesson.

- Do the games that are related to this lesson: How do you imagine it?, Puppets, Acrostic, Flags.

QUESTIONS

CHAPTER 8
1. What was Philip doing in the city of Samaria? (8:5)
Proclaimed the Messiah

2. Who was always with Philip? (8:13)
Simon.

3. Who prayed for those in Samaria to receive the Holy Spirit? (8:15)
Peter and John.

4. According to Acts 8:20, what did Simon think?
That he could buy the gift of God with money.

5. What was the Ethiopian doing when Philip approached him? (8:28)
He was sitting in his chariot reading the Book of Isaiah the prophet.

6. What did the Spirit say to Philip? (8:29)
"Go to that chariot and stay near it."

7. What happened after Philip baptized the Ethiopian? (8:39)
* the Spirit of the Lord suddenly took Philip away.
* the Ethiopian went on his way rejoicing.

SAUL IS TRANSFORMED
Lesson 6

BIBLICAL PASSAGE: Acts 9:1-31

KEY VERSE: "But the Lord said to Ananias, "Go! This man is my chosen instrument to proclaim my name to the Gentiles and their kings and to the people of Israel" (Acts 9:15).

TEACHING OBJECTIVES - To help the children:

1. Know that God transforms what we are and our way of life.
2. God enables us to be his instruments.

BIBLICAL COMMENTARY

Saul's story of transformation is one of many dramatic conversion stories in Acts. This type of experience does not happen to everyone, but the story reminds us that God reaches people through a multitude of methods.

Saul's conversion happened after his personal encounter with the risen Christ. After his conversion, Saul became part of the same community of believers that he persecuted.

Ananias and most of the believers in Damascus knew about Saul and feared him. However, the Lord used Ananias to heal Saul and to welcome him into the community of believers. Barnabas encouraged the other disciples to accept Saul, and he became a friend and supporter of Saul's ministry.

Because of Saul's past lifestyle, God was able to use him in unique ways to share the gospel with Jews, and, later, to share it with Gentiles.

Saul suffered persecution because he refused to yield to the pressure of Christ's adversaries. Those who discounted Jesus as Lord and Christ also resisted Saul's testimony. It is common for faithful followers of Jesus to experience opposition, since people who seek positions of power often disregard Jesus and his message.

Even though Saul had a dramatic experience of conversion, he did not stop growing as a disciple of Christ. His growth continued throughout his life.

Each day he learned more about who God wanted him to be. As other believers taught him more about Jesus, his zeal for proclaiming the faith to all people grew. Previously, he brought fear and death to people, but after he met Jesus he proclaimed hope and life.

As Christians, God asks us to do many of the same tasks as those early believers. Ananias and Barnabas teach us to encourage one another despite our fears. From Saul, we learn to proclaim hope and light to those who live in fear and darkness. Like so many other early believers, most of whom are never named in Acts, we learn our job is to be faithful witnesses to the on-going work of Christ.

WORDS OF OUR FAITH

Faith — Trust in God that leads people to believe in what He has said, depend on Him and obey Him. Faith is trust in action.

Saul — Known also as Saul of Tarsus, Saul was a Roman citizen who dedicated part of his life to persecuting Christians. After converting to Christianity, he became a prominent leader of the early church. After his conversion he was called Paul.

Gentiles — Those who are not Jews.

Church — People who know and love God and his Son, Jesus. The church is all believers everywhere. The "primitive church" is a term that refers to the early believers, contemporaries of Paul.

The Way — The Christian faith. At first the word "Christians" was not used to describe those who believed in Jesus. The first Christians called themselves "followers of the Way". In John 14:6, Jesus says that He is "the way."

OPENING ACTIVITY

For this activity you will need the following:

- Pieces of paper and pen/pencil (one for each child)
- Before class, write the words of Acts 9:15 on pieces of paper. Prepare enough for all students. Give them the verses.

Say: *God has the power to change a person's life. In today's lesson, we will learn from a man who changed completely. This verse of the Bible tells us about that change.*

Read Acts 9:15. Discuss the meaning of each word or phrase that children don't know.

Ask the children to divide into groups of two to help each other memorize the verse. Tell them to take turns reading a word of the verse. The first child reads the first word, then the other reads the second. The first reads the third word and the other reads the fourth. Continue until the children can say the whole verse without looking at the paper.

Say: *In today's lesson, Saul changed his ideas and beliefs about Jesus. You can take the paper with the verse home and show it to someone else.*

BIBLE LESSON

1. Removing the Tiger's spots (9:1-19a)

Sure, you remember Saul. We met him in the stoning of Stephen: Stephen's killers "laid their coats at the feet of a young man named Saul" (7:58); and "Saul approved of their killing him" (8:1). Then we read that Saul "began to destroy the church. Going from house to house, he dragged off both men and women and put them in prison (8: 3). In this passage we read that Saul was "still breathing out murderous threats against the Lord's disciples" (v. 1).

* Choose one or more of the children and cover their eyes. After a few minutes, remove the blindfolds and ask them what it felt like; this is to help the children understand what happened to Saul. Then ask the following questions:

1. In v. 15, what did the Lord say that Saul was?

2. And in v. 17, what did Ananias do with Saul.

It's important that you emphasize to the children the importance of the Holy Spirit.

2. The hunter is hunted (9:19b-31)

After his conversion, Saul didn't waste time: "at once he began to preach in the synagogues that Jesus is the Son of God" (v. 20). This man who had been the terror of the Christians was now their defender.
But what Saul had done to the Christians previously had consequences.

* Read Luke 9:18-27 and then answer these questions:

1. What do you think the Christians in Damascus thought of Saul?

2. After his escape from Damascus, Saul traveled to Jerusalem. What did he find there? (v. 26)

SUGGESTED ACTIVITIES

- Continue with the glossary of Words of our Faith.

- Add to the list the characters, places and objects that appear in this lesson.

- Do the games that are related to this lesson: Crossword puzzle.

QUESTIONS

CHAPTER 9:1-31
1. Who breathed murderous threats against the disciples of the Lord? (9: 1)
Saul

2. What did Jesus say to Saul? (9:4-5)
Saul, Saul, why do you persecute me?

3. What was Saul for three days? (9: 9)
He was blind, and did not eat or drink anything.
4. According to Acts 9:10, to whom did the Lord speak to in a vision?
Ananias
5. Where was Saul for some days with the disciples? (9:19b)
In Damascus.

6. To whom did Barnabas describe in detail what had happened to Saul? (9:27)
To the apostles

7. Who intended to eliminate Saul? (9:29)
The Hellenistic Jews

8. In the meantime, what happened in the church of Judea, Galilee and Samaria? (9:31)
- It enjoyed a time of peace and was strengthen.
- It lived in the fear of the Lord
- It was encouraged by the Holy Spirit and grew in number.

TO EAT OR NOT TO EAT

Lesson 7

BIBLICAL PASSAGE: Acts 9:32 - 10:1-23

KEY VERSE: "He and all his family were devout and God-fearing; he gave generously to those in need and prayed to God regularly" (Acts 10:2).

TEACHING OBJECTIVES - To help the children:

1. Know that God can change our way of thinking.

BIBLICAL COMMENTARY

God sometimes used visions to reveal his will and purpose. Two visions occur in this story. Cornelius was a Gentile soldier who lived in Caesarea. Acts describes him and his family as "devout and Godfearing" (10:1) Cornelius was a man with authority whose devotion to God was displayed in acts of generosity and faithful prayers.

Early believers prayed three times a day (at nine o'clock in the morning, noon, and at three o'clock in the afternoon). So, it is not surprising to see that Cornelius was praying. During his prayer time, he saw an angel of God who told him to send for Peter. The story does not tell us if Cornelius experienced any doubt at this request, but he must have known that Jews were not allowed to enter the home of a Gentile. Yet, Cornelius faithfully obeyed God.

In the next part of the story, Peter also saw a vision. While in Joppa, he had a vision of a sheet descending from heaven with all kinds of animals in it—unclean and clean animals. Based on Jewish law, Peter knew that he was not allowed to eat anything that was labelled as unclean.

However in this vision God spoke to Peter and told him, "Do not call anything impure that God has made clean" (10:15). Peter did not understand what the vision meant, but he would find out very soon.

The men that Cornelius sent arrived. Because of the vision, Peter did two things that Jewish law did not allow: he invited the men to spend the night, and the next day, he went to Cornelius' house. God was breaking down cultural barriers that separated Jews and Gentiles.

The Holy Spirit worked simultaneously in the lives of Cornelius and Peter to spread God's message to new people. Because both of these men were obedient and receptive to new ideas, many people believed in God..

WORDS OF OUR FAITH

Righteous — to be in right relationship with God and to obey him because of that relationship. To be righteous is to be like Christ in thoughts, words, and actions.

The Law of Moses — the rules that God gave to Moses to teach the people of Israel how to live. Sometimes, the Law of Moses is simply called the Law. These rules are found in the first five books of the Old Testament.

OPENING ACTIVITY

For this activity you will need the following:

- Pieces of paper (one for each student)
- Pen or pencil
- A sheet, a large cloth or a large piece of paper
- Paper to make a small sign.

Before class, write on some pieces of paper "Jewish" and write "Gentile" on others. Hand out a piece of paper to each child. Try to have an equal number of both words. On another piece of paper, write "Cornelius." Place a sheet, cloth or large paper on the floor. On another paper, write the words "Kingdom of God." Put this sign in the center of the cloth/paper.

Say: The Jews were people who believed in God and followed Jewish laws. The Jews considered themselves the people of God and part of the kingdom of God. Everyone who was not a Jew was a Gentile.

Give the papers to the children. Point to the fabric and the sign.

Say: *I want everyone who has the word "Jewish" to stand on this cloth. In the New Testament time, there were Gentiles who knew about God, followed their laws and prayed to Him every day. Cornelius was one of them.* Ask the person holding the paper with Cornelius' name to stand on the fabric.

Say: *In today's lesson, we will learn how God worked through Cornelius so that Peter could learn an important lesson. Keep your papers. At the end of the lesson, we'll see how the Gentiles became part of the kingdom of God. Then everyone can join the "Kingdom of God" on the cloth.*

BIBLE LESSON

1. The Church continues to expand (9:32-43)

When the Christians dispersed to the regions of Judea and Samaria (8: 1), the apostles stayed in Jerusalem. But not for long. The Church was growing rapidly in Judea and Samaria and needed the help and supervision of the apostles.

In this first passage, we find Peter in Lydda, a town near the coast of Judea on the Mediterranean Sea, where he healed Aeneas, a paralytic confined to his bed. Then Peter went to Joppa, where a bigger miracle happened.

* Read 9: 32-43 and answer these questions:

1. Look at the words of Peter in the healing of Aeneas (v. 34). To whom did Peter give the credit for the miracle?
2. Some have speculated that Tabitha was not dead, but in a coma (very sick). They say that the miracle was Peter's ability to diagnose the coma and get rid of it. What do you think?
3. If Peter, as an agent of the Holy Spirit, could raise Tabitha from death, couldn't he also raise Stephen? Why do you think he didn't?

2. To eat or not to eat (10:1-23)

Sometimes we try to make others like us. But that goal isn't good. We can love and value a person because he was created by God.

A better goal for us is to want to be like Christ. Believers may be very different in appearance and culture. But, these same believers may find that they have common attitudes and actions when guided by the Holy Spirit.

* Ask the children to read the passage and answer the following questions:

1. In your opinion, why did the angel tell Cornelius to send men to ask Peter to come to his house?
2. Why did Peter worry when the voice told him to kill and eat the animals he saw on the canvas?
3. What would the world be like if we were all the same? If everything were of a single color or a single form? Or if there was only one kind of food to eat? In your opinion, why did God create such a variety of people?
4. How do you treat people who are different from you? How do you think God wants us to treat those who are different?

SUGGESTED ACTIVITIES

- Continue with the glossary of Words of our Faith.
- Add to the list the characters, places and objects that appear in this lesson.
- Do the games that are related to this lesson: Puzzles, Acrostic, Puppets, Musical Roulette.

QUESTIONS
Acts 10:1-23

1. What was the name of the paralytic that Peter found in Lydda? (9:32-33)
   Aeneas
2. What did Tabitha do? (9:36)
   She was always doing good and helping the poor.
3. What did Peter tell Tabita? (9:40)
   Tabitha, get up.
4. Who gave generously to those in need and prayed to God regularly? (10:2)
   Cornelius
5. Where Simon the tanner's home? (10:6)
   By the sea
6. According to Acts 10:8, where did Cornelius send two of his servants and a devout soldier?
   To Joppa
7. Who went up on the roof to pray? (10:9)
   Peter
8. What did the voice say to Peter when he replied, "I have never eaten anything impure or unclean." (10:14-15)
   Do not call anything impure that God has made clean.

GOD DOESN'T HAVE FAVORITES

Lesson 8

BIBLICAL PASSAGE: Acts 10:24 – 11:26

KEY VERSE: "Then Peter began to speak: 'I now realize how true it is that God does not show favoritism'" (Acts 10:34).

TEACHING OBJECTIVES - To help the children:

1. Understand that God's salvation is available for everyone.

BIBLICAL COMMENTARY

Peter's vision of the clean and unclean animals was very mysterious. He trusted God and went to Cornelius' house. Once again, Peter had the opportunity to preach to a large crowd. This sermon was different from the one he preached on the day of Pentecost. It was not filled with quotes from the Jewish scriptures. Instead, Peter talked about who Jesus was and how he accepts anyone who believes in him (10:34).

This was something new, because the Jewish people believed fervently that they were not like other people. They believed that God favored them over everyone else in the world. Peter, a devout Jew and at the same time a devout Christian, preached a new message: God does not show favoritism. God's Spirit interrupted Peter. These Gentiles received the Holy Spirit just like the Jewish believers did at Pentecost. Then, they were baptized by Peter.

Because of the vision that God had sent him, Peter began to understand that God's salvation through Christ is for all people. Peter wrote about this in his own letters, 1 and 2 Peter. God revealed his desires to Peter, and Peter was courageous enough to accept what he heard and tell others about it.

God had an ever-expanding mission to accomplish. It started in Jerusalem, but God wanted to spread the good news about Jesus to the ends of the earth. Through the power of the Holy Spirit, God helped Peter understand this mission. The Gentiles, who once were outsiders, were invited to share in Israel's blessings.

The mission to the Gentiles continued when Barnabas visited the church in Antioch. Barnabas invited Saul to join him to teach these new believers what it meant to follow Jesus. They stayed in Antioch for a year, and believers there were the first ones to be called Christians.

WORDS OF OUR FAITH

A Christian — a person who renounces sin, accepts Jesus Christ as Savior and Lord, and obeys him. This experience is also called "being born again."

OPENING ACTIVITY

For this activity you will need the following:

- 10-12 pieces of paper in two colors (if you do not have color paper, draw an asterisk on the back of one of the groups of papers).
- Pen or pencil.
- Before class, divide the words of Acts 10:34-35 into short phrases.

Write a phrase on each piece of paper. Make two sets of papers: one of each color. Hide the papers in different places in the room.

In class, divide the children into two teams. Say: *Today's memory verse is Acts 10: 34-35.* Read the verse, then tell the teams that the words of the verse are on papers hidden in the room. Tell the teams to look in the room, but only take the papers of the color of their team. When they find all the pieces, they should put the sentences in the correct order. Then ask each team to repeat the verses three times.

Say: *These verses teach us an important lesson that Peter had to learn. They changed Peter's idea about who could be followers of Jesus. Until that team, the disciples preached only to the Jews. After this, the disciples took the gospel to the Gentiles.*

BIBLE LESSON

1. The Holy Spirit and the gentiles (10:24-48)

Tell the children the story contained in this passage and then discuss these questions with the children:

1. What were the main points of Peter's message to the family and friends of Cornelius?

2. Compare what happened to the Gentiles in this story (10:44-46) and what happened to the Jews on the day of Pentecost (2:1-4).

3. Why were the Jewish believers who were with Peter stunned when the Holy Spirit was poured out on the Gentiles?

4. What kind of man was Barnabas? Do you know people today who are like Barnabas?

Say: *In Antioch, Barnabas and Saul continued to meet with the people and teach them. It was there that the believers were called Christians for the first time. People recognized that they were different because they followed Christ. Think for a moment about your identity. People should be able to recognize us as followers of Christ in the same way they identified those early believers.*

2. Peter convinces the church leaders (11:1-18)

What had happened in Caesarea was so important that the news reached Jerusalem before Peter got there. In fact, by the time Peter got home, the Jewish leaders were already furious. Simply entering a Gentile's house and eating with him was a violation of the Law. Peter would have to answer for his actions. And what a response he gave!

* Ask the children to read Peter's defense in 11:1-18 and then answer the following:

1. Why do you think Luke again tells the whole story he had already written earlier in the book?

2. The center point of Peter's argument is in verse 17. Read this verse again and write it in your own words.

SUGGESTED ACTIVITIES

- Continue with the glossary of Words of our Faith.
- Add to the list the characters, places and objects that appear in this lesson.
- Do the games that are related to this lesson: Puzzles.
- Do an interview with Peter. Ask an adult to represent Peter and answer questions about Peter's activities in this Bible lesson. Let the children be the reporters who ask Peter about his activities and thoughts. If possible, provide a list of questions to the adult before the class. Give the questions to the children during class. If there is time, allow the children to ask their own questions.

QUESTIONS
Acts 10:24 – 11:26

1. What did Cornelius do when Peter arrived at the house? (10:25)
   He met him and fell at his feet in reverence.

2. Who does not show favoritism? (10:34)
   God

3. According to Acts 10:44, what happened while Peter was still talking?
   The Holy Spirit descended upon all who were listening to the message.

4. Who found out that the Gentiles had also received the Word of God? (11:1)
   The apostles and the believers in all Judea.

5. Who criticized Peter when he went to Jerusalem? (11:2)
   The circumcised believers.

6. What did Peter see in what looked like a large sheet? (11:6)
   Four-footed animals, wild beasts, reptiles and birds.

7. According to Acts 11:16, what had the Lord said?
   John baptized with water, but you will be baptized with the Holy Spirit.

8. What has God also granted to the Gentiles? (11:18)
   Repentance that leads to life

PETER'S PRISON BREAK

Lesson 9

BIBLICAL PASSAGE: Acts 12 – 13:1-12

KEY VERSE: "Right then three men who had been sent to me from Caesarea stopped at the house where I was staying." (Acts 11:11)

TEACHING OBJECTIVES - To help the children:

1. Understand that God is always with us, regardless of what happens.

2. God answers our prayers.

BIBLICAL COMMENTARY

James 5:16 says, "The prayer of a righteous man is powerful and effective." Throughout the book of Acts we see how true this statement is. It is especially evident in today's two stories as we see the results of the believers' prayers.

First, God heard the believers' prayers, and amazingly rescued Peter from prison. Peter's miraculous deliverance came just in time, since he was sentenced to die the next morning. In faith, the church believed and trusted in God's power.

However, even if Peter was killed (like Stephen was), their prayers would not have been ineffective or unimportant. God is honored when people demonstrate faith in difficult circumstances. See Hebrews 11 for more examples of this.

The second story is found in chapter 13. The church in Antioch gathered to worship and fast. During this time, the believers discerned the Spirit's call on Barnabas and Saul to preach the gospel to other nations. After the church received this direction, they prayed for Saul and Barnabas, and then sent them to begin their new mission. The phrase "laying on of hands" (13:3) shows that they were supported by the church to be their representatives.

As believers called by God to do his work, we need the prayers and support of other Christians in order to be effective. Peter, Saul, and Barnabas had this support. When we pray, we demonstrate trust in God's power, even when God displays power in a way that we don't understand.

WORDS OF OUR FAITH

The Passover — the annual Jewish feast that celebrates God's deliverance of the Israelites from slavery in Egypt. See Numbers 9:4-5 for more information.

To execute — to put to death, especially as a legal penalty.

To fast — to abstain from something, usually food, or certain types of food, as a type of spiritual discipline. Christians use times of fasting to pray and focus on God.

Prayer — a conversation with God that includes both talking and listening. We can pray anytime, anywhere, about anything.

OPENING ACTIVITY

For this activity you will need the following:

- Paper strips (8 per child, approximately 20 x 3 cms.)
- Adhesive tape or stapler

Before class, make the model of a paper chain. Make the first link forming a circle and securing it with adhesive tape or staple. Insert another strip into the circle and secure it. Continue until you have a chain of eight links. These should be large enough in diameter so that children can put their hands on the first link and the last.

In class, show your chain to the children. Help them make their own chains.

Let the children put the chain on their wrists while they study the Bible passage of today's lesson. When Peter's chains are broken in history, instruct the children to break theirs.

Say: *In today's lesson, Peter is in jail. He is chained. The soldiers are there to make sure that he doesn't escape. Only God could save Peter's life.*

BIBLE LESSON

1. Peter is in jail ... again! (12:1-25)

In this passage we read about the persecution of the Church in Jerusalem by King Herod, including the murder of the second martyr of Christianity and the arrest of Peter.

* Tell the children Acts 12:1-25 and ask them to answer these questions:

1. Who was the second Christian who lost his life for the faith? What do you know about him?
2. While Peter was in prison, what were the other Christians doing in Jerusalem? Was it effective?
3. What was the ruin of Herod and the cause of his death?
4. Despite all the persecution, what was happening with the Church (v. 24)? What does this tell you about the Word of God?

2. On your marks, get set, go! (13:1-12)

Did Paul have the intention of being a missionary? We don't know. But here we read that the church in Antioch, while they were worshiping the Lord and fasting, was instructed by the Holy Spirit to "Set apart for me Barnabas and Saul for the work to which I have called them" (v. 2). From the order of the names, and from Barnabas' position in the church, it is clear that he was going to be the leader of the trip.

After praying and fasting, the church of Antioch commissioned the missionaries and sent them out.

* Ask the children to read about the first part of their trip in 13:1-12 and then answer the following:

1. Who was with Barnabas and Paul as an assistant? (v. 5)
2. Where did the missionaries first preach when they arrived in Salamis on the island of Cyprus? What does this mean?
3. Notice that in verse 9, we first read Paul's name. It was common for Jews to have two names. The first was his Hebrew name; the second was his Greek name. So far the Hebrew name "Saul" has been used. But from now on, the Greek name "Paul" will be used. Do you think this change of names means something?

4. In this passage we find two sorcerers. Search for the word in a dictionary. (And think about the sorcerer we read about in 8:9-24.) Why do you think the sorcerers were attracted and opposed to the work of the church so much?

SUGGESTED ACTIVITIES

- Continue with the glossary of Words of our Faith. Add to the list the characters, places and objects that appear in this lesson.
- Do the games that are related to this lesson: Crossword Puzzles.
- Invite an adult to tell the children how God answered a prayer.

QUESTIONS

Acts 12 – 13:1-12

1. Who did Herod command to be killed with the sword? (12:2)
James, John's brother

2. What was the church doing while Peter was in prison? (12:5)
The church was earnestly praying to God for him.

3. How did Peter sleep in jail? (12:6)
Between two soldiers, bound with two chains.

4. How did the angel awaken Peter? (12: 5)
He struck him on the side.

5. Who came out to answer when Peter knocked on the front door? (12:13)
A servant named Rhoda.

6. When did the Holy Spirit say: "Set apart for me Barnabas and Saul for the work to which I have called them"? (13:2)
While they were worshiping the Lord and fasting.

7. Who was with the governor Sergius Paulus? (13:6-7)
A false Jewish prophet named Bar-Jesus.

8. What happened to Elymas the magician when he opposed Barnabas and Saul/Paul? (13:8-11)
He went blind.

TO THE ENDS OF THE EARTH

Lesson 10

BIBLICAL PASSAGE: Acts 13:13 – 14:28

KEY VERSE: "Strengthening the disciples and encouraging them to remain true to the faith. 'We must go through many hardships to enter the kingdom of God,' they said." (Acts 14:22)

TEACHING OBJECTIVES - To help the children:
1. Understand that following Jesus sometimes includes sacrifices.
2. Have the courage to experience difficulties for the sake of Christ.

BIBLICAL COMMENTARY

Beginning in Acts 13, we reach a key point in Luke's story. So far the action has focused on Jerusalem and the countries bordering on Palestine. The Early Church, under Peter's leadership, had been fulfilling Jesus' promise that they would be witnesses "in Jerusalem, and in all Judea and Samaria" (1:8), mainly with the Jews.

Now the center of attention changes. For purposes of balancing the book we will see the Church spread to the ends of the earth (1:8). We will also see how the emphasis of the central figure of Peter changes to Paul, with a corresponding change from Jerusalem as the center of the Church to Antioch, the "headquarters" of Paul.

Today's Scripture begins in Antioch where the saints, who gathered to pray and fast, received instructions from the Holy Spirit: "Set apart for me Barnabas and Saul for the work to which I have called them" (13:2). We don't know If these two Christians were planning to become missionaries, but the Holy Spirit did have plans for them.

The church in Antioch commissioned the missionaries and they departed on what we know today as the first of Paul's three missionary journeys, a trip that would last approximately three years.

WORDS OF OUR FAITH

Crippled - Someone who has permanently damaged any part of their body, especially any of their extremities (arms, legs).

Difficulties — Situations, circumstances or obstacles difficult to overcome.

OPENING ACTIVITY

For this activity you will need the following:

- One sheet of paper for each child

Help the children make a paper boat, and then during the lesson ask them to write down on the boat the places where Paul and Barnabas arrived.

Say: *Today we will learn about Paul's first trip and how he and Barnabas encouraged the new Christians and helped organize the early church.*

BIBLE LESSON

1. Another Antioch, another sermon (13:13-52)

From Cyprus, the missionaries sailed to Perga, on the coast of what is now known as Turkey. From there they traveled inland to Antioch of Pisidia. This is not the same Antioch where they began their journey and where their headquarters were.

Antioch of Pisidia was at 1,100 meters above sea level, and to make this trip they had to cross the Taurus Mountains on one of the most difficult roads in all Asia Minor, a road known because there were many robbers. Here John Mark leaves them to return home. Remember this incident, we'll talk about it later.

Paul's sermon in Antioch is the only complete sermon of his that Luke records in Acts. After the sermon, something happened that influenced the rest of Paul's ministry.

* Ask the children to read this passage and summarize the three most important ideas of Paul's sermon.

2. The missionaries travel inland (14:1-20)

In their previous stop of Antioch, Paul and Barnabas were persecuted and thrown out (13:50), so they traveled inland to Iconium. As was their custom, they first spoke in the synagogue. The success of their ministry there was met with a plot to kill them, so once again they had to go, this time to Lystra and Derbe.

* Ask the children to read 14:1-20 and answer the questions:

1. In Lystra, Paul healed a crippled man. Why did Paul single out this man above the others? (v. 9)

2. How did the crowd respond to the healing of this man? (vv 11-13)

3. In verses 15-17, we have Paul's first message to a totally pagan audience. How does it differ from his previous sermon and from the others we have read in Acts?

4. Once again, Paul was persecuted. This time they stoned him, leaving him for dead. Who instigated this persecution (13:50; 14:2, 19)? Why do you think they were against Paul's ministry?

3. Back home (14:21-28)

After a stop in Derbe, Paul and Barnabas returned to Lystra, Iconium and Antioch before returning home to Antioch in Syria.

* Ask the children to read this passage and then answer these questions:

1. Returning to the cities where they were persecuted and physically attacked seems crazy. Why did they do it? (vv.22-23)

2. The missionaries told the newly converted that they "must go through many hardships to enter the kingdom of God" (v. 22). Certainly, Paul and Barnabas had experienced this, but why say something so discouraging to new believers?

3. When the missionaries returned home, they reported on their trip. Look at the words of verse 27: "all that God had done through them." What does this tell us about these two men?

SUGGESTED ACTIVITIES

- Continue with the glossary of Words of our Faith.

- Add to the list the characters, places and objects that appear in this lesson.

- Do the games that are related to this lesson: Where was Paul?, Biblical Geography, Modern Day Bible, Drama.

- Mark Barnabas and Paul's journey on a map.

QUESTIONS

Acts 13:13 – 14:28

1. What did John preach? (13:24)
Repentance and baptism

2. What is written in the second psalm? (13:33)
You are my son, today I have become your father.

3. According to Acts 13:43, what happened when the assembly was dismissed?
Many of the Jews and devout converts to Judaism followed Paul and Barnabas, who talked with them and urged them to continue in the grace of God.

4. According to Acts 13:52, the disciples were ....?
Filled with joy and the Holy Spirit.

5. According to Acts 14:4, how were the people of the city divided?
Some sided with the Jews, others with the apostles.

6. To whom did Paul say, "Stand up on your feet!"? (14:8, 10)
A man crippled from birth who lived in Lystra.

7. What is necessary to enter the kingdom of God? (14:22)
Must go through many hardships.

8. Two-part question, what did they appoint in each church, and with what did they commit them to the Lord? (14:23)
Elders. They committed them to the Lord with prayer and fasting.

9. To whom did God open the door of faith? (14:27)
The Gentiles

THE ESSENTIAL THING

Lesson 11

BIBLICAL PASSAGE: Acts 15

KEY VERSE: "God, who knows the heart, showed that he accepted them by giving the Holy Spirit to them, just as he did to us." (Acts 15:8)

TEACHING OBJECTIVES - To help the children:

1. Know what other Christians expect from us.

2. Understand that in Christianity, we grow in different ways, and we must accept ourselves as we are and others as they are.

BIBLICAL COMMENTARY

Being that our culture is different than in those days, it's difficult for us to understand some of the Jewish laws mentioned in Acts. The new believers in Antioch had no Jewish background. There was some confusion about which parts of the Jewish law all believers should respect, regardless of their background. The letter sent by the Jerusalem church answered their questions, but raises some questions for us today.

• Why were these four laws so important? These laws refuted the common pagan practices associated with polytheism (worship of many gods) in Antioch. The new believers had to believe only in Jesus. By avoiding these practices, the new Christians gave testimony to others about the inner change that Christ was making in them. These laws also helped maintain peace between Jewish and Gentile believers.

• Did they have to obey other laws (the Ten Commandments, the Sermon on the Mount, etc.)? Yes. The Gentiles still had to live according to the moral principles of the law and the Ten Commandments. At first, God wrote the law on stone tablets. The prophets showed that God also wrote the law on the hearts of Jews and Gentiles (Jeremiah 31:33). Jesus gave new meaning to the law by creating a covenant

based on internal transformation. This means that God first changes our purposes, and then our actions, when we decide to obey Him in truth. Although we are not bound to follow the same laws of the Old Testament, our hearts must be transformed by the moral principles on which those laws are based. In the Sermon on the Mount, Jesus taught his followers to obey God from the heart, not just to obey the laws.

Gentile believers in Antioch were to follow such principles. These requirements helped them internalize the law.

They also help us understand what it means to follow the commands of Jesus, not because they are a requirement but because we love God.

This lesson also speaks of a disagreement between Paul and Barnabas. Christians may sometimes disagree. However, they should try to find peaceful solutions. Christians should never allow their disagreements to interfere with the preaching of the gospel.

WORDS OF OUR FAITH

Pagan - Someone who does not believe in God. Some pagans worship many gods. Others do not worship any.

Sermon on the Mount — The Biblical passage in Matthew 5-7. It is the most extensive teaching of Jesus recorded in the Bible. In this sermon, Jesus describes how Christians should live in relationship with God and with others.

OPENING ACTIVITY

For this activity you will need the following:

• Paper and pencil for each child

Before class, prepare a list of five categories of what children like (for example: food, games, books, animals and places). In the class, distribute the papers and pencils. Ask the children to write their favorite object or animal in each category.

Then choose two volunteers. Ask each volunteer to say which is their favorite item in the first category and explain why.

Say: *Each one of you thinks that your favorite article is the best one. Could someone convince you that you are wrong and that he or she is right? If not, can you agree that they think differently about this issue and you can still be friends? If so, tell each other: "We agree that we think differently and we can still be friends."*

Allow these volunteers to return to their seats and call two others. Continue until everyone has read their answers. Encourage the volunteers to say: *"We agree that we think differently and we can still be friends".*

Say: *In today's lesson, we will learn that Paul and Barnabas had a disagreement. We'll see how they solved it.*

BIBLE LESSON

1. The problem (15:1-5)

We read that during Paul's first missionary journey many Jews, many God-fearing Gentiles (Gentiles who studied and worshiped with Gentiles) and many pagans had converted to Christianity. Although we would have been happy for this evangelistic impulse "to the world", some Jewish Christians in Jerusalem were very angry.
There were two, maybe three, opinions about it. Paul and Barnabas obviously believed that God accepted Gentiles in the Church as they were, honoring their faith in Christ, regardless of their status as Gentiles. However, some of the Christian Jews in Jerusalem strongly believed that the Gentiles should first convert to Judaism. And surely there were those who were between these two positions, accepting the Gentile Christians in the Church with a type of "associated" or "second class" membership (maybe until they converted to Judaism).

The Hebrew nation had always accepted the Gentiles in their community if they did two things: submit to circumcision and live under the Old Testament Law. (Circumcision is a minor surgical procedure done on male babies shortly after birth, or in this case, male adults - for the Jews it was a symbolic act that indicated their obedience to the Law).

2. The council makes a decision (15:6-21)

When the leaders of the Church met with Paul and Barnabas in Jerusalem, there was "a long discussion." We can imagine that Luke is being careful with his words. There was probably a heated discussion.

Three key people addressed the group: Peter, Paul and Barnabas (speaking as one), and James.

* Ask the children to read verses 6-21 and then answer the following:

1. When Peter spoke, what previous incident did he refer to?

2. Observe the words of Peter: "God ... made a choice" (v. 7); "God. . . He showed" (v. 8); "He did not discriminate" (v. 9). Why do you think Peter used those words?

3. What was Paul and Barnabas' contribution to the discussion? (v.12)

4. James was the next to speak. He was not the brother of John, one of the first apostles. Remember that he had been martyred (12:2). This is James, the brother of Jesus, who converted and by this time had become the leader of the congregation in Jerusalem. He used an Old Testament quote. Summarize the quote.

5. Finally, James agreed that the Gentiles should be admitted into the Church without becoming Jews first, as long as they followed four rules. The four requirements were suggested so that Gentile Christians could have communion with Christian Jews without offending them or violating their vows. What were the four requirements?

3. Write it! (15:22-29)

After James spoke, the Church decided to accept his position. To avoid misunderstandings, they wrote down their decision and then sent some representatives to explain the document in person.

* Read the verses and list the requirements.

4. Letter received (15:30-35)

Because of the kind and conservative way in which Luke describes this incident, one might have the impression that it was a small matter. But in reality, this was one of the greatest crises in the Church. If it had not been resolved, it would have divided the Church into two parts, the Gentiles and the Jews. Reading between the lines, we have the idea that all those involved were very careful to treat the matter in a logical and compassionate manner, without threats or authoritarian pronouncements.

* Ask the children to read these verses and answer the following questions:

1. How did the Gentiles of Antioch receive the letter and the messengers?

2. What did Judas and Silas, the representatives of the Jerusalem church, do in Antioch?

SUGGESTED ACTIVITIES

*   Continue with the glossary of Words of our Faith.

*   Add to the list the characters, places and objects that appear in this lesson.

*   Ask the children, with the help of their parents, to read passages at home to reinforce this study.

QUESTIONS
Acts 15

1. Who set out to teach the brothers: Unless you are circumcised, according to the custom taught by Moses, you cannot be saved."? (15:1)
Some who had come from Judea to Antioch.

2. What did Paul and Barnabas say when they passed through Phoenicia and Samaria? (15:3)
How the Gentiles had been converted.

3. Who stated the following: "The Gentiles must be circumcised and required to keep the law of Moses."? (15:5)
Some believers who belonged to the party of the Pharisees

4. Who knows the human heart? (15:8)
God

5. Who had a good reputation among the brothers? (15:22)
Judas (called Barsabbas) and Silas

6. What requirements are mentioned in Acts 15:29?
Abstain from food sacrificed to idols, from blood, from the meat of strangled animals and from sexual immorality.

7. According to Acts 15:36, what did Paul say to Barnabas?
Let us go back and visit the believers in all the towns where we preached the word of the Lord and see how they are doing.

8. Why didn't Paul think it was wise to take John Mark? (15:38)
He had deserted them in Pamphylia and had not continued with them in the work.

PAUL IN PHILIPPI

Lesson 12

BIBLICAL PASSAGE: Acts 16

KEY VERSE: "They replied, 'Believe in the Lord Jesus, and you will be saved—you and your household.'" (Acts 16:31)

TEACHING OBJECTIVES - To help the children:

1. God always gives the opportunity to receive his gift of salvation.
2. It is important to understand and fulfill God's will.

BIBLICAL COMMENTARY

In today's lesson, we read about three people who were influenced for good by the gospel in Philippi: Lydia, a girl who predicted the future, and a jailer.

In Philippi, Paul met some women gathered at the river. Lydia, one of these women, was a successful businesswoman, a dealer in purple cloth. Purple cloth was commonly sold to wealthy people or to those associated with royalty. Socially, Lydia was a success, but her spiritual needs were only satisfied through Christ. Lydia's conversion and hospitality established her home as the base for continued missions in Philippi.

There was a slave girl who had a spirit by which she predicted the future. In Jesus' name, Paul commanded that the demon come out of her. The exorcism prevented her owners from continuing to make a profit, so Paul and Silas were beaten and imprisoned. This is one of many times that Paul would endure suffering because of his faith in Jesus, as predicted in Acts 9:16.

In prison, Silas and Paul sang hymns and prayed to God, while the other prisoners listened. They worshiped, even though they were suffering.

Just like Paul and Silas, we can help others to see that God is at work in our lives regardless of our circumstances. When we praise God during adversity, it is a great testimony to the power of the Holy Spirit.

An earthquake provided an opportunity for escape. However, for Paul and Silas, it provided another opportunity to share the gospel. Not only did they save the life of the jailer, they pointed him to eternal life in Jesus.

Paul faithfully followed the Spirit's guidance, even though he led Paul in unexpected directions. Paul obeyed God by going to Macedonia instead of Phrygia and Galatia. While looking for a special place of prayer, Paul witnessed to Lydia. While preparing for a day of ministry, Paul freed a possessed girl. This caused him to be jailed. While in jail, he was able to witness to other prisoners as well as to the jailer.

Through all of these unexpected events, Paul exuded confidence and faith in the Holy Spirit. We would be wise to follow Paul's example, proclaiming the message of Jesus no matter our circumstances, wherever we are.

OPENING ACTIVITY

For this activity you will need the following:

- Objects to prepare an obstacle course
- A small scarf or towel to blindfold

Before class, prepare an obstacle course: a course with objects that the child must go around or jump over to reach the end. If possible, prepare this track in another room so that children who participate cannot see the obstacles before the activity begins. You can use cardboard boxes, bags filled with old newspapers, or something else you have. (When preparing the track, consider the safety of the children.) Provide a scarf or small towel to blindfold.

In class, choose a volunteer to walk the obstacle course. Take the volunteer and the other children to the track.

Say: *In our lesson today, Paul wanted to go to Bithynia, but the Holy Spirit stopped him. After a vision from God, Paul decided to go instead to Macedonia. Today, our volunteer represents Paul. He tried to decide where God wanted him to go. You can help direct our volunteer through this track so that he does not trip or fall.*

Choose another volunteer to give oral directions to the blindfolded child. If you have time, allow other children to try the obstacle course.

Say: *God gives us the Holy Spirit to help us know what to do. God led Paul to the places he wanted Paul to be.*

BIBLE LESSON

1. Choose your team (16:1-5)

At the end of chapter 15, the story of this journey begins with a painful incident involving ministry personnel. Before leaving this story, we need to find out how it ends. Paul mentioned in his later writings both John Mark (whom he simply calls "Mark") and Barnabas.

* Read together with the children 1 Corinthians 9:6; Colossians 4:10; 2 Timothy 4:11; and Philemon 24.

1. What do these references tell you about Paul's later situation with these two men?

2. Barnabas was replaced by Silas as Paul's partner. In 16:1-5, we learn that Paul also found a young helper as a replacement for John Mark. Who was this replacement and what do we know about him from these verses?

2. A change of plans (16:6-10)

So far, all of Paul's trips have been in Palestine and the region we know today as Asia Minor (now Turkey). Apparently he intended to continue his missionary work in that region. But when he was in Troas, he received new orders for his itinerary. Do not miss the importance of these verses.

"Macedonia" is part of the current Greece (not to be confused with the Republic of Macedonia). That region was not only the cultural and intellectual center of the Western world, it was also in Europe, not Asia.

Ask the children to read these verses and answer the following questions:

1. From what you know about history, why was it so important that Paul's travel plans changed from Asia to Europe? (Why is it important for you?)

2. In verse 7, we read that when Paul wanted to go to Bithynia, "the Spirit of Jesus would not let him." We are not given any further explanation.

How do you think the Holy Spirit communicated this to Paul?

3. After Paul's vision of the Macedonian man, Luke tells us that they immediately prepared to leave for Macedonia. What does this tell us about Paul?

3. The Philippian jail (16:11-40)

From Troas, where Paul received the vision of the Macedonian man, the group traveled to Philippi, a Roman colony. (The church that Paul had founded there later received a letter, which we know as the Epistle to the Philippians). Here we discover the influence that the gospel had on three very different people: a wealthy business woman, a slave girl, and a Roman jailer.

According to Luke's account, the first person converted in Europe was a woman named Lydia. As a seller of "purple cloth", an expensive fabric in the ancient world, she was probably very rich. Luke tells us that "the Lord opened her heart to respond to Paul's message" (v. 14). What do you think that means?

The next person we meet in Paul's ministry was a young slave girl who predicted the future. Why do you think Paul was upset about this young woman's behavior? Was she making a scene? Was she telling lies? Or could it be something else?

As Paul expelled the evil spirit from the young woman, her masters sent Paul and Silas to prison. There the missionaries found the third Philippian character, a Roman jailer. What event led to his conversion?

* Help the children memorize verse 31, for it contains one of the clearest and simplest statements of the gospel in the Bible.

SUGGESTED ACTIVITIES

- Add to the glossary of the Words of our Faith the characters, places and objects that appear in this lesson.
- Choose games related to this lesson: Tell me the Person, Where was Paul?, Biblical Geography, Chest of memories, How do you imagine it?, Explosions, Flags, Answer and Draw, Emotion-art, Charades.
- Make decorative signs with the text of this lesson and ask the children to place it in a special place in their home.

QUESTIONS

Acts 16

1. Why did Paul circumcise Timothy? (16:3)
Because of the Jews who lived in that region, for they all knew that his father was Greek.

2. What vision did Paul have during the night? (16:9)
A man of Macedonia standing and begging him, "Come over to Macedonia and help us."

3. Name the two characteristics of the city of Philippi: (16:12)
- *A Roman colony*
- *The leading city of the district of Macedonia.*

4. Who was Lydia? (16:14)
A purple cloth seller from the city of Thyatira who worshiped God.

5. What was the young slave who had a spirit of divination shouting? (16:17)
These men are servants of the Most High God, who are telling you the way to be saved.

6. What did the girl's masters do when they realized that they had lost hope of making money? (16:19)
They seized Paul and Silas and dragged them into the marketplace to face the authorities.

7. Being in the dungeon, what did Paul and Silas do around midnight? (16:25)
They were praying and singing hymns to God.

8. Who said it, who did they say it to, and what was the reaction: "Don't harm yourself! We all are here!"? (16:28-29)
Paul, to the jailer, The jailer asked for light, rushed in and fell trembling before Paul and Silas.

9. Who asked, to whom, and what was the response: "Sirs, what must I do to be saved?" (16:30-31)
The Jailer, to Paul and Silas, and the answer was: "Believe in the Lord Jesus; and you will be saved – you and your family."

ANOTHER JOURNEY
Lesson 13

BIBLICAL PASSAGE: Acts 17

KEY VERSE: "The God who made the world and everything in it is the Lord of heaven and earth and does not live in temples built by human hands." (Acts 17:24)

TEACHING OBJECTIVES - To help the children:

1. Understand that God sends us to the world to share his love.

2. Not be religious, but love God and obey Him because we know Him through the Holy Scriptures.

BIBLICAL COMMENTARY

While Paul was in Athens, he saw many idols throughout the city. There was even one labelled as "TO AN UNKNOWN GOD." Athens was an elite city, home to a university and intellectuals who valued ideas and learning.

Paul debated Epicurean and Stoic philosophers. Epicureans pursued pleasure in order to achieve happiness. They sometimes used self-denial as a way to achieve long-term happiness. Stoics taught people to live in accordance with nature and to be emotionally unaffected by things.

Paul preached that the "Unknown God" that they worshiped was in fact, the one, true, and living God. He explained that God created the world, that he gives us life and breath, and that we are his children.

The gospel message that Paul preached challenged many of the ideas that were culturally acceptable to the Athenians. The Athenians were different than the Jewish people to whom Paul preached before. This new audience did not know the Jewish Scriptures. So, Paul taught them using language they understood. He used familiar metaphors to help them begin to understand God. He even used quotes from their literature to describe God. He spoke to these educated philosophers in a manner that appealed to their intellect. He presented the gospel in a captivating manner.

The Athenians longed for something authentic to worship. They searched for something that would give their lives meaning and purpose. We know that their minds were open to the idea of a new God since they acknowledged an "Unknown God."

In the same way, many people in our world today search for God, but they don't know how to describe him. It's our responsibility to find ways to share the message of Jesus with all people, not just those with similar backgrounds. Jesus is the one for whom they search, and only he is able to fulfil their desire to know God.

WORDS OF OUR FAITH

The Sabbath — the day God set aside for rest, worship, and doing good. For Jews, the Sabbath is the seventh day (Saturday.) Christians celebrate the Lord's Day (Sunday) as their Sabbath, since this is the day that Jesus rose from the dead.

A missionary — a person called by God and sent by the Church to take the gospel to people of other countries or cultures.

An idol — anything that is worshiped instead of God, or loved more than God. The city of Athens was full of idols made of gold, silver, or stone.

The Areopagus — a hill in Athens where a council of philosophers met to discuss philosophical issues. Paul spoke to this group about Jesus' resurrection.

OPENING ACTIVITY

For this activity you will need the following:

- One piece of paper and a pencil for each child

Before class, write this statement on the paper for each child: "I am willing to go wherever God asks me to go and tell people about Jesus." On the bottom of the paper, draw a line for the child's signature.

In the class, say: *We have studied the trips that Paul made to many cities. Why did Paul travel to those cities?* (God asked Paul to talk about Jesus to the people.)

What is a missionary? (Someone who travels to another country or culture to talk to people about God and his plan of salvation through Jesus.)

In what ways would the world have been different if Paul had stayed in Jerusalem and refused to travel?

(People in other parts of the world wouldn't have heard of Jesus - God could have chosen someone else to spread the gospel, but perhaps he wouldn't have had Paul's courage and determination.)

Say: *God could ask one of you to leave his city and travel to another place to proclaim the gospel. If God asked you to do that, would you answer "yes"?*

Distribute the papers and pencils. Read the statement; Then pray, asking God to help the children be willing to talk to others about Jesus, either where they live or in another part of the world. Encourage the children to write their name if they are willing to share the good news of Jesus, wherever they go, and to anyone whom God asks them to speak. Some children will sign immediately, but others may want to do it later. Ask them to take the paper home and keep it in their Bible or other safe place.

Say: *We give thanks to God for Paul and other missionaries who spread the gospel to many areas of the world.*

BIBLE LESSON

1. Paul on tour in Greece (17:1-34)

Now we are going to quickly cover the rest of Paul's second missionary journey. In these verses we will read about Paul's visits to some of the largest cities in Greece: Thessalonica, Athens and Corinth, among others. In Thessalonica and Corinth, Paul founded congregations to which he later wrote 1 and 2 Thessalonians, and 1 and 2 Corinthians of our New Testament.

In this passage, we observe that Paul continued his habit of visiting the Jewish synagogues when he arrived in each city (17:2, 10, 17). We also note that he was very persecuted by the Jews (17:5, 13).

* Ask the children: *why do you think Paul was still trying to evangelize the Jews despite how badly they treated him?*

In 17:16-34, we have Paul's visit to Athens, a city that we always identify with Greek culture and philosophy. There Paul was saddened by the worship of the idols he observed. In verses 22-31, we can read his sermon to the pagans.

* Compare this sermon with the one Paul gave to another group of pagans in Lystra (14:15-17). How are they similar? How do they differ? How do they differ from other sermons given to Jewish audiences in the book of Acts?

Briefly summarize Paul's approach to his ministry in each of these cities he visited, and the results he achieved:
• Thessalonica (17: 1-9)
• Berea (17: 10-15)
• Athens (17: 16-34)

SUGGESTED ACTIVITIES

• Continue with the glossary of Words of our Faith. Add to the list the characters, places and objects that appear in this lesson.

• Do the games related to this lesson: Tell me the Person, Where was Paul?, Bible Bingo, How do you imagine it?, Modern Day Bible, Flags, Drama, Breaking News.

• Make decorative signs with the key verse of this lesson and ask the children to place it in a special place in their homes.

QUESTIONS
Acts 17

1. What was necessary for the Messiah? (17:3)
The Messiah had to suffer and rise from the dead.

2. Who recruited bad characters? (17:5)
Jealous Jews

3. What did the authorities demand to free Jason and the others? (17:9)
They had to post bond.

4. What greatly distressed Paul? (17:16)
See that the city was full of idols

5. Why did they examine the scriptures every day? (17:11)
To see if what Paul said was true.

6. According to Acts 17:18, what did Paul preach to them?
The good news about Jesus and the resurrection.

7. What did the inscription on the altar say? (17:23)
To an unknown god

8. Who is the God who made the world and everything in it? (17:24)
The Lord of heaven and earth.

9. According to Acts 17:31, what has God set?
A day when he will judge the world with justice.

TEACHING AND PREACHING

Lesson 14

BIBLICAL PASSAGE: Acts 18

KEY VERSE: "The God who made the world and everything in it is the Lord of heaven and earth and does not live in temples built by human hands." (Acts 17:24)

TEACHING OBJECTIVES - To help the children:

1. Understand that God encourages us to share his love, even though others reject us.

BIBLICAL COMMENTARY

Luke introduces us to fellow ministers who helped Paul: Priscilla, Aquila, and Apollos.

When many in the Jewish population in Corinth refused to repent, Paul absolved himself of the responsibility to teach them. He focused on the Gentiles because they were responsive to the message. A vision from the Lord encouraged Paul to remain in Corinth, and he stayed there for 18 months. During that time, he had many opportunities to share the message about Jesus and to build relationships with people.

When Paul left Corinth, Priscilla and Aquila joined him. The three had much in common. They were business partners and shared a vocation. While they were in Ephesus, they met Apollos, a church planter from Egypt. Apollos was intelligent and knew the Scriptures. However, he didn't know the entire story of Jesus. So, Priscilla and Aquila discipled him. Apollos used what he learned, and he travelled to Achaia proclaiming and defending the faith.

In 1 Corinthians, Paul mentioned the work of Priscilla and Aquila (16:19) and Apollos (3:6, 9). He said that he planted the seed of the gospel in Corinth, but Apollos came behind him and watered it by encouraging the believers and teaching them. God made it grow.

Ministry is not one person's job. It takes many people to do the job correctly. In today's lesson, we learn:

- We must be gracious when we admonish others. Aquila and Priscilla taught Apollos that his understanding of Jesus was not complete. Yet, they did this in private, so that they wouldn't embarrass him.
- We all have a role in ministering to those around us and sharing the gospel with them.

At times it is easy to become discouraged if someone doesn't accept Christ. However, we can find peace in the knowledge that God can and will use all of us to help lead others to him.

Just as he used Apollos to water the seed Paul planted, he can use us either in planting the seed of faith or helping it grow.

OPENING ACTIVITY

For this activity you will need the following:

- Blackboard and chalk, or whiteboard and markers

Before class, write this sentence on the board: "However, Paul obeyed God."

In class, say: Today we will look at some of Paul's difficult experiences. I will read a sentence, and then I want you to read what is written on the board. Repeat these words after I read each sentence.

Read these sentences and wait for the children to respond.

- In Jerusalem, Christians feared Saul. (However, Paul obeyed God.)
- In Salamis, a magician wanted to prevent Saul from evangelizing the ruler. (However, Paul obeyed God.)
- In Antioch of Pisidia, some Jews caused trouble for Paul and Barnabas. (However, Paul obeyed God.)
- In Iconium, some Jews stirred up the Gentiles and planned to mistreat and stone Paul. (However, Paul obeyed God.)
- In Lystra, some people stoned Paul and dragged him out of the city. (However, Paul obeyed God.)
- Paul and Barnabas had a disagreement about John Mark. (However, Paul obeyed God.)

- Paul wanted to go to Mysia, but the Holy Spirit told him to go to Macedonia. (However, Paul obeyed God.)
- In Philippi, the magistrates locked Paul and Silas in jail. (However, Paul obeyed God.)
- In Thessalonica, the Jews started an uproar against Paul. (However, Paul obeyed God.)
- In Athens, some believed in Jesus, but others made fun of Paul. (However, Paul obeyed God.)
- In Corinth, the Jews opposed Paul and began to blaspheme, so he addressed the Gentiles. (However, Paul obeyed God.)

Say: *Paul suffered many difficult situations. Maybe you also face ridicule or difficult situations. Don't give up. Perhaps your friends or family members don't appreciate what you say or do as a Christian. However, like Paul, keep obeying God.*

BIBLE LESSON

1. I continued the tour of Greece (18:1-17)

In the previous chapters, Paul undertook a trip to Greece where he visited several places on his journey to Corinth, a city in which Paul founded a congregation.

Like the previous lesson, you can see how Paul visited the Jewish synagogues (18:4, 19), and again was persecuted by the Jews (18:6, 12).

* Ask the children to briefly summarize what Paul's focus was in this city and what the results were.

2. John's baptism (18:23-28)

Although the first verse speaks of Paul, the rest of the section deals with something that happened at the same time in Ephesus, one of the churches Paul had founded on a previous trip.

An Egyptian Jew named Apollo arrived in Ephesus. Obviously he had heard the gospel before, since "he had been instructed in the way of the Lord, and he spoke with great fervor and taught about Jesus accurately" (v. 25). However, he only knew part of the story.

* Ask the children to read these verses and answer the questions:

1. According to verse 25, what was missing from Apollo's information?

2. What do you think Paul meant by "John's baptism"? You'll find more details in Matt. 3:11.

SUGGESTED ACTIVITIES

- Continue with the glossary of Words of our Faith. Add to the list the characters, places and objects that appear in this lesson.
- Choose games related to this lesson: Tell me the Person, Where was Paul?, Finish the story, Modern Day Bible, Collage, Drama.

QUESTIONS
Acts 18

1. Who did Paul find in Corinth? (18:2)
A Jew named Aquila

2. Why had Aquila and Priscilla come from Italy? (18:2)
Because Claudius had ordered all Jews to leave Rome.

3. What did Paul do when they arrived in Macedonia? (18:5)
Preached

4. Who believed in the Lord with all his family? (18:8)
Crispus (the synagogue leader)

5. Who was the governor of Achaia? (18:12)
Gallio

6. On whom did everyone turn and beat in front of the proconsul? (18:17)
Sosthenes (the head of the synagogue)

7. What did Paul do because of a vow he had made? (18:18)
He had his hair cut off.

8. What congregations did Paul visit one by one? (18:23)
The congregations of Galatia and Phrygia

9. What was the only baptism that Apollo knew? (18:25)
John's

10. What did Priscilla and Aquila do with Apollo? (18:26)
They invited him to their home and explained to him the way of God more adequately.

11. What did Apollo prove from the Scriptures? (18:28)
That Jesus was the Messiah.

RIOTS AND MIRACLES

Lesson 15

BIBLICAL PASSAGE: Acts 19:1 – 20:12

KEY VERSE: "In this way the Word of the Lord spread widely and grew in power." (Acts 19:20)

TEACHING OBJECTIVES - To help the children:

1. Understand that the Holy Spirit empowers us to do amazing things.

BIBLICAL COMMENTARY

Paul's ministry to the Ephesians evoked high emotions: positive emotions towards the Spirit, and deep-seated anger towards Christianity.
When Paul arrived in Ephesus, the believers there had not experienced the power of the Holy Spirit. Paul asked them some questions and then taught them about Jesus and the Holy Spirit. He baptized the new believers.

While in Ephesus, God performed miracles through Paul: healing diseases and driving out evil spirits. These acts were evidence of the Spirit's work through Paul.

However, anger rose among the local silversmiths, who made a lot of money creating silver idols of the local god. Paul's preaching threatened their way of life, both religiously and financially. They tried to stop Paul's message, but were unsuccessful.

Despite the uproar in Ephesus, Paul continued to travel and preach the message of Christ. He understood that persecution and trials would be a part of his life.

WORDS OF OUR FAITH

Repentance — the act of turning away from sin and turning toward God. To feel sorry for sin, to ask for forgiveness, and to live for God.

OPENING ACTIVITY

For this activity you will need the following:

- A map of the world
- A map of your country
- A map of your city

In class, read Acts 1: 8 to the children. Repeat the meaning of "witness".

Say: *Name the places mentioned in Acts 1:8.* Allow the children to respond. *Jerusalem is a city. Judea and Samaria are countries. The ends of the earth represents the other parts of the world. If you obey what this verse says, you'll testify of the Lord in your city, in your country, and in other parts of the world.*

How can you witness to people in your city? (You can testify to family and friends, to people in stores, to those you see at school and in other parts of the city.)

How can you witness to people in other parts of your country? (You can testify to relatives or friends who live in other parts of the country, perhaps when you go on vacation to another city.)

How can you witness to people in other countries? (You can write letters to missionaries. When you give offerings for missions, you help missionaries take the gospel to many other countries.)

You can testify to people in your city, your country and in other parts of the world. You can obey what Acts 1:8 says.

BIBLE LESSON

1. Paul in Ephesus (19:1-41)

Chapter 19 of Acts talks about some of the events of Paul's three-year stay in Ephesus, one of the great cities of Asia Minor.

* Read the chapter to the children and have them answer the questions:

a. Once again we find disciples with an incomplete understanding of the gospel. Like Apollo, these disciples understood the "baptism of John" (vv.3-4). How did John define his baptism? (v. 4)

b. What did these disciples lack? (v. 2)

c. Read again Acts 2:1-4; 8:14-17; 10:44-46. How are these verses related to 19:1-7?

d. Notice that Luke speaks of Christianity simply as "the Way" in verse 9. Look for similar references in Acts 9:2; 19:23; 22:4; 24:14, 22. What do you think Luke meant when referring to Christianity in this way?

2. From the window (20:1-12)

When Luke describes the last part of Paul's third missionary journey, he seems to hurry, and leaves out many details.

In this chapter, however, he pauses long enough to tell us the story of an evening in the church and of Eutychus, a young man who fell asleep in the service (does he remind you of anyone?). Why do you think Luke gave himself the space to tell this story?

SUGGESTED ACTIVITIES

- Continue with the glossary of Words of our Faith. Add to the list the characters, places and objects that appear in this lesson.
- Do the games related to this lesson: Tell me the Person, Breaking News.

QUESTIONS
Acts 19:1 – 20:12

1. What happened when Paul laid hands on the twelve men? (19:6)
The Holy Spirit came on them, and they spoke in tongues and prophesied.

2. According to Acts 19:11, what did God do through Paul?
Extraordinary miracles

3. Who was the guardian of the temple of the great Artemis and of her image, which fell from heaven? (19:35)
The city of Ephesus

4. Who said goodbye and left to go to Macedonia? (20:1)
Paul

5. Where was Paul three months? (20:2-3)
In Greece

6. Where was Sopater from? (20:4)
Berea

7. Why did Paul keep talking until midnight? (20:7)
Because he had to leave the next day

8. Where was Eutychus sitting? (20:9)
In the window

9. According to Acts 20:12, how did they take the young man home?
Alive

PAUL'S AMAZING RACE - 1

Lesson 16

BIBLICAL PASSAGE: Acts 20:13 - 21:16

KEY VERSE: "However, I consider my life worth nothing to me; my only aim is to finish the race and complete the task the Lord Jesus has given me— the task of testifying to the good news of God's grace." (Acts 20:24)

TEACHING OBJECTIVES - To help the children:

1. Understand that God has entrusted us with the work of proclaiming the gospel to others.

BIBLICAL COMMENTARY

Paul was faithful to the gospel even though it cost him a lot. He suffered numerous hardships in order to proclaim the truth of Jesus. Wherever he went, Paul expected to suffer on behalf of the message.

In Paul's final exhortations to the church in Ephesus, he reminded them of his example. He worked hard to supply his own needs. In the same way he exhorted the Ephesians to work hard, to help the weak, and to share the gospel. He reminded them not to seek monetary rewards but to recognize the value of their relationships. See Matthew 5:1-12 for ways that Christians experience blessings from God.

One of the characteristics that defines Christians is their service to those on the margins of society. The stories of Acts demonstrate how believers shared their lives with each other, including their resources. This is the mission that Paul emphasized to the Ephesians.

Paul described his trials as a reminder that those who follow Jesus might encounter great hardships. It is the Holy Spirit who enables the follower to endure and persevere.

Paul's report helped further to reconcile his troubled relationship with the leaders of the church in Jerusalem. His ministry to the Gentiles did not contaminate the faith.

On the contrary, extending the message to the Gentiles demonstrated the great grace and mercy of Jesus. The good news about Jesus was that God continually sought to bring all people to himself. We share in God's mission when we share Jesus with others.

WORDS OF OUR FAITH

Grace — everything that God does for us including his love, mercy, forgiveness, and power at work in our lives. God freely gives us his grace because he loves us, not because we deserve it.

An exhortation— a short speech conveying urgent advice or recommendations. Acts includes several exhortations from Paul to churches that he visited.

OPENING ACTIVITY

You will need these items for this activity:

• A piece of paper and pencil for each child

Before class, choose a task that you complete regularly (for example: preparing to go to work, shopping for groceries, planning, or helping children with their school work). Make a list of the steps you perform to complete the task.

Say to the class, *Here is a task that I do regularly. Here are the steps I take to complete that task.* Read your list. Distribute the paper and pencils. Instruct the students to think of a task that they do each day. They will create a list of the steps to complete the task. Let volunteers read their lists. Ask each volunteer, *If you omitted any of the steps, would you finish the task?* Allow time for the children to discuss the question.

Read Acts 20:24. Say, *Paul was determined to complete the task that God gave to him.*

Ask a volunteer to read Acts 13:46-47. Say, *In these verses, Paul told the Jews that they rejected his message about Jesus. Therefore, God sent Paul to the Gentiles to preach the gospel to them. Paul reported to the leaders of Ephesus and Jerusalem. He told them that he wanted to complete the task that God gave to him. Paul travelled to many cities.*

He preached the gospel and followed the guidance of the Holy Spirit.

Take time to pray with the children. Ask God to help the children to do whatever he wants them to do.

BIBLE LESSON

1. Paul says good-bye to Asia Minor (20:13-38)

In this passage, Luke describes an emotional farewell to us. In verses 17-38, we find Paul's farewell to the leaders of the church in Ephesus, where Paul had spent three years.

Verses 22-24 give us a foreshadowing of what will happen.

* Ask the children to read the passage and then answer:

1. What do these verses tell us about Paul?

2. What does verse 34 say about Paul?

2. Towards Jerusalem (21:1-16)

These verses narrate the last leg of Paul's third missionary journey. Verses 4 and 10-12 are an echo of something we read in the previous section. What is it?

It is very important that in this section you notice what Paul's reaction was to the prophecy that he was going to be arrested in Jerusalem? (v. 13)

SUGGESTED ACTIVITIES

- Continue with the glossary of Words of our Faith.
- Add to the list the characters, places and objects that appear in this lesson.
- Do the games related to this lesson: Bible Bingo.

QUESTIONS

Acts 20:13 - 21:16

1. According to Acts 20:19, how did Paul serve the Lord?
With great humility and tears

2. Who had proclaimed God's will without hesitation? (20:27)
Paul

3. Who told Paul not to go to Jerusalem? (21:3-4)
The disciples of Tyre

4. The daughters of whom prophesied? (21:9)
The daughters of Philip the evangelist

5. When did a prophet named Agabus come down from Judea? (21:10)
After they had been in Caesarea a number of days

6. What was Paul willing to do for the name of the Lord Jesus? (20:13)
Not only to be bound but also to die in Jerusalem.

7. Who brought them to the home of Mnason? (21:16)
Some of the disciples from Caesarea

PAUL'S AMAZING RACE - 2

Lesson 17

BIBLICAL PASSAGE: Acts 21:17 – 22:21

KEY VERSE: "You will be his witness to all people of what you have seen and heard." (Acts 22:15)

TEACHING OBJECTIVES - To help the children:

1. Understand that when God wants us to speak in his name, he will tell us what to say.

BIBLICAL COMMENTARY

The Roman commander rushed to prevent a riot. He ordered his soldiers to arrest Paul and bind him with two chains. He did this for Paul's safety. This was the third time that the authorities came to the aid of Paul: first in 18:12-17 and then in 19:23-41. These instances served to further preserve and to spread the gospel.

Paul asked the commander for permission to speak to the people. With his consent, Paul addressed the crowd to explain his actions.

Paul called them "brothers and fathers" in their own language of Aramaic. Hearing this familiar language caused them to listen intently. He gave a testimony of his family, his tradition, and his heritage. He identified himself as a Jew. He showed that he was a credible speaker due to his knowledge of Jewish law and customs.

Clearly, he did not dismiss their concerns as trivial. He sought to establish a connection with them based on their native language, their common upbringing, and the fact that, like them, he was a religious zealot. Paul understood their zealous behavior because he also persecuted Christians before his conversion. The distinction he made to the crowd was that they were zealots for the law, and he was now a zealot for God. Paul tried to explain to them that when he became a follower of Christ, he did not forsake Judaism.

His new faith led him to follow the God of Judaism as the one who also reaches out to the Gentiles. Once again, Paul defends his actions. The extension of God's grace to the Gentiles is not his idea, but God's. This explanation did not appease the crowd. Instead, they were appalled that Paul would claim that this was God's initiative.

The crowd wants to lynch Paul, so they tried to prove that he committed the sin of blasphemy speaking inappropriately about God. In their way of thinking, it was impossible to consider that God did not favor Israel in an exclusive manner. Paul's preaching and actions, if they were truly of God, would destroy their understanding of God and their relationship to him. They were angry at Paul, but if Paul was telling the truth, they must be angry at God instead. This was an unacceptable situation for them. The only other option was to recognize that God accepts Gentiles and to submit to his will.

The commander ordered the soldiers to flog Paul. The commander was surprised when Paul identified himself as a Roman citizen, and he ceased Paul's punishment. It was illegal to flog a Roman citizen not found guilty. According to Roman law, all Roman citizens were excluded from any type of degrading forms of punishment such as flogging and crucifixion.

Paul shows us that witnessing is not complicated. We share our story of what we were like before God saved us. We then can share about the difference God made in our lives. God gave Paul the courage to share his story of salvation. Even though the crowd rejected Paul's message, God gave him the courage to speak and taught him what to say. God will do the same for us as we share our story with others.

WORDS OF OUR FAITH

To flog — to beat severely with a scourge. A scourge is a leather whip with metal attached to the ends.

A zealot — A zealot was a member of a patriotic group of Jews in Judea during the time of the Early Church. They wanted to overthrow Roman rule. They vigorously and violently resisted the Roman government.

To testify — to tell about something. People who believe in Jesus tell others about him, how he is God's son and wants to be our Savior. A testimony is when Christians tell about their experience with God.

OPENING ACTIVITY

You will need these items for this activity:

- Paper for each child
- Pencil for each child
- Chalkboard and chalk or marker board and markers

Before class, write a brief biography about your life. Include your birth place, family, places you lived, school, and work. If you have one, bring a childhood picture of yourself to share with the class. Write about your church experience, such as the age when you began to attend church, conversion, and spiritual milestones.

Write on the board these topics: birth, places you lived, family, school, work or hobbies, church.

In class, say, *A biography is the story of someone's life. A biography contains the information listed on the board and perhaps other topics too. Here is a brief biography about me.* Read your biography.

If time permits, let the children write information about each of the topics on the board. If time is short, ask volunteers to stand and to talk briefly about each of the topics.

Say, *In this study, we saw that Paul had the opportunity to witness to others. He witnessed when he told his life story and his spiritual story. He told how he became a follower of Jesus. You can witness to others when you tell your story and your love for Jesus.*

BIBLE LESSON

1. New in the City? You're arrested! (21:17-36)

When Paul arrived in Jerusalem, he immediately reported to the church and told them how he had done on his last trip. The church leaders praised God for Paul's success, but they immediately told him about a problem: there were rumors that Christian Jews were encouraged to ignore Jewish laws and traditions.

* Read the first part of this passage to the children (v. 17-26) and then have them answer the following:

1. Was the rumor true?

2. What did the leaders suggest he do?

3. Why do you think Paul agreed to accept the rite of purification, even when he was innocent?

4. How important is it for us to adapt to those within the church whose standards are different from ours?

The second portion of this passage reveals that this conciliatory plan didn't work. After some Jews from Asia (probably from Ephesus) saw Paul, they started an uproar.

* Read verses 27-36 and have the class answer these questions:

1. The penalty for bringing Gentiles to the Temple was death. Was Paul guilty of that accusation?

2. Why do you think the Jews were so upset with Paul?

3. Although Luke speaks of this briefly, don't forget the violence against Paul in verses 30-31. Had it not been for the Roman soldiers, they would have killed him with their blows. What do you think Paul thought while all this was happening?

2. Facing the mob (21:37-22:21)

When the soldiers rescued Paul from the mob, he asked for permission to speak with those who were about to kill him.

Paul spoke to the Roman commander in Greek, the soldier's language, but he spoke to the mob in Aramaic, their language. What can we deduce from this?

In 22:3, Paul tells the crowd that his teacher had been Gamaliel. Do you remember that name? Review Acts 5:34-39. What do you think Paul learned from his teacher?

In 22:4-16, Luke tells the story of Paul's conversion, a story he told us in chapter 9, why do you think he tells us the story again?

Verse 21 tells the last thing Paul could say to the mob before they interrupted him. Starting from what Paul mentioned in his defense, what do you think he was going to say?

SUGGESTED ACTIVITIES

- Continue with the glossary of Words of our Faith.

- Add to the list the characters, places and objects that appear in this lesson.

- Place folded papers in the classroom with words such as: Family, friend, neighbor, etc. and ask the children to stand on a piece of paper, then ask them to pick it up and read what it says.

  Tell the children that Paul always took the opportunity to talk about Jesus. Now the children should say the name of a relative, friend, neighbor, etc. who they will tell about Jesus

QUESTIONS

Acts 21:17 – 22:21

1. Who praised God for what He had done among the Gentiles? (21:20)
James and all the elders

2. According to Acts 21:23, what do the four men have to fulfill?
Vow

3. According to Acts 21:26, where did Paul enter to announce the date on which the purification period would end?
Into the temple.

4. Who saw Paul in the temple when the seven days were almost over? (21:27)
Some Jews from Asia

5. Where was Paul born? (22:3)
In Tarsus of Cilicia

6. Who was Paul arresting and throwing into jail? (22: 4)
Both men and women.

7. According to Acts 22:17, where was Paul praying?
At the temple in Jerusalem

8. According to Acts 22:21, what did the Lord say to Paul?
Go; I will send you far away to the Gentiles.

A MURDEROUS PLOT

Lesson 18

BIBLICAL PASSAGE: Acts 22:22 – 23:35

KEY VERSE: "The following night the Lord stood near Paul and said, "Take courage! As you have testified about me in Jerusalem, so you must also testify in Rome." (Acts 23:11)

TEACHING OBJECTIVES - To help the children:

1. Trust in God in spite of the difficulties, since he cares for us and frees us.

BIBLICAL COMMENTARY

Again, Paul is in trouble and God delivers him.

The commander in Jerusalem arranged for the Sanhedrin to gather in order to determine why the Jews opposed Paul's preaching. Paul made it clear that he was obedient to God by preaching about the resurrection of the dead. In anger, the high priest ordered those next to Paul to hit him. This gave Paul the opportunity to display his knowledge of the law. Then he revealed his status as a Pharisee and his belief in the resurrection.

The Pharisees and Sadducees were political and religious rivals. The Sadducees did not believe in resurrection, angels, or spirits. However the Pharisees believed in them.

These two groups sought the attention of the Jewish people. They often cared more about their position and being right than they did about God's approval. This worked to Paul's advantage since the violent arguing prompted the commander to take Paul back to the safety of the barracks.

The next night, the Lord visited Paul. He told him to be brave. Paul was going to Rome, the capital of the empire, to testify about Jesus. Paul was encouraged and reminded that God is sovereign, even during chaotic circumstances.

In Jerusalem, Paul's life was dangerous. Paul's nephew reveals a plot to the Roman officials. The Jews planned to kill Paul. The commander listened to Paul's nephew. Since the commander believed Paul was innocent, he went to great measures to keep him safe. Paul's life was spared and he was able to continue spreading the gospel.

WORDS OF OUR FAITH

Sovereign — To be sovereign means to have the power to rule without limits. God is sovereign. His power to rule is not limited in any way, except when he limits himself.

OPENING ACTIVITY

You will need these items for this activity:

• Pieces of paper

• Pen

• Chalkboard and chalk or marker board and marker

Before class, write each of the parts of matching pairs on separate pieces of paper:

• Jonah | a huge fish

• The Israelites | the Red Sea

• The three Hebrew men | the fiery furnace

• David | Goliath

• Elijah | the prophets of Baal on Mount Carmel

• Joseph | prison

If the children are not familiar with these stories, choose other ones that talk about faithful people in difficult situations.

Write the memory verse on the board.

In class, say, *The Bible tells of many people whom God rescued from difficult situations.* Distribute the cards with people and difficult situations. Ask the children to find the person who holds a card that matches what they have. When the children find the correct partner, have them read together the words of Acts 23:11. When all the matches are complete, ask the class to read together Acts 23:11.

Say, *God still watches over us today. He helps us when we experience difficult situations. We can pray and ask for his help.* Ask the children if they are aware of any people in difficult situations. Perhaps one of the children or one of the families experienced sickness or a tragedy. Take time to pray for these situations.

BIBLE LESSON

1. Let the trial begin (22:22-23:11)

Since the Israel of that time was an occupied territory, there was a double system of justice. Israel itself was a theocracy (a country ruled by God and religious leaders) that was dependent on a system run by the Sanhedrin or Council, the "supreme court" of Judaism. But the power of the Council was limited by the Roman government. For example, they could not legally impose the death penalty or execute someone. The real power in Israel lay in the Roman army and the Roman justice system.

After they arrested Paul, he was in the custody of the Roman government. But since the accusations were of a religious nature, not civilian, the first step was an appearance before the Council or Sanhedrin.

Before Paul's appearance before the Sanhedrin, the Roman commander decided to interrogate him with lashes. But before he started torturing him, Paul told the soldier that he was a Roman citizen. Whipping a Roman citizen was illegal. Did Paul inform the soldier about his citizenship from fear of being flogged? If not, what would be the reason?

Paul's behavior before the Council has given the scholars many headaches. First, he addressed the group as "parents and brothers" (22:1). This would have been considered in that time as a lack of respect. Why do you think Paul did that? Paul's response to the high priest (verse 3) is very hard. Why did Paul respond in this way? (v 4-5).

One of the biggest causes of disagreement between the Sadducees and the Pharisees (the two groups that made up the Council) was the resurrection of the dead. The Sadducees believed that when a person died, that was all. But the Pharisees believed in the resurrection and life after death. There are those who believe that when Paul mentioned the subject of the resurrection, he was simply trying to divert attention from his case and divide the Council. Do you think that was what he was trying to do?

2. The Plot is entangled (23:12-35)

Although Paul was in Roman custody, the Jews were still plotting something.

* Read this section with the children and answer the questions:

1. Why do you think the 40 men (v. 12-13) were so determined to kill Paul?
2. Do you think that the fact that Paul's nephew happened to be in Jerusalem and found out about the conspiracy was coincidental, or was it God at work?
3. The head of the Roman government in Israel was in Caesarea, a little over 96 kilometers from Jerusalem. The Roman commander, who was probably fed up with the matter, sent Paul there to attend to his case.

Read the letter he sent to the Roman governor Felix, in verses 26-30. Does the soldier tell the whole truth?

SUGGESTED ACTIVITIES

- Continue with the glossary of Words of our Faith. Add to the list the characters, places and objects that appear in this lesson.
- Do the games related to this lesson: Breaking News; Help the Missionaries.

QUESTIONS

Acts 22:22 – 23:35

1. What did Paul have by birth? (22:25-28)
Roman citizenship.

2. What has Paul done with all good conscience? (23:1)
Fulfilled his duty to God in all good conscience to that day

3. Who ordered those who were with him to hit Paul in the mouth? (23:2)
The High Priest Ananias

4. According to Acts 23:6, what did Paul know?
That part of the council was Sadducees and the other part Pharisees

5. According to Acts 23:13, how many men were involved in the conspiracy?
More than forty

6. Where did the son of Paul's sister go when he heard about the plot? (23:16)
To the barracks (and warned Paul).

7. Where did Commander Claudius Lysias send Paul accompanied by a detachment? (23:23-35)
To Caesarea, to Governor Felix.

PAUL'S LIVING TESTIMONY

Lesson 19

BIBLICAL PASSAGE: Acts 24, 25, 26

KEY VERSE: "So I strive always to keep my conscience clear before God and man." (Acts 24:16)

TEACHING OBJECTIVES - To help the children:

1. Witness the work of God in their lives.
2. Understand the importance of having a clear conscience.

BIBLICAL COMMENTARY

Festus was the Roman governor of Judea. He administered Roman law. Festus was newly appointed, so he requested the assistance of King Agrippa and Queen Bernice, Agrippa's sister, to help solidify his report to Caesar about Paul. Festus hoped to absolve himself of responsibility by appealing to Agrippa.

Paul's witness to King Agrippa included the statement from Jesus (on the road to Damascus), "It is hard for you to kick against the goads" (26:14). Herders used sticks with sharpened points called goads to prod cattle in the right direction. So, the proverb that Paul quoted was about futile resistance. The animal resisting only ended up hurting itself. Before his conversion, Paul fought against God. Paul recognized that it was actually to his detriment to resist God. He changed his mind and began serving Jesus rather than persecuting him.

Festus's interruption of Paul's speech in 26:24 actually served to emphasize Paul's last point: the resurrection of Jesus. It is the hope in the resurrection that inspired Paul to preach the good news to the Gentiles, which resulted in upsetting the established Jewish tradition. Festus thought that Paul's belief in the resurrection was crazy.

Agrippa noted that Paul's conflict with the Jews was religious in nature, and separate from the legal matters of Rome. Paul chose to appeal his case to the Roman emperor. Otherwise, Agrippa and Festus could free him.

Paul's journey was almost over. He started in Jerusalem, then he spread the gospel all over the province of Judea. He declared the story of the risen Jesus to kings and emperors along the way. Eventually he would preach in Rome, the center of the ancient world, and then to the ends of the earth.

WORDS OF OUR FAITH

Judea — the homeland of the Israelites. Shortly before the time of Jesus, it was conquered by the Romans and became part of their empire.

OPENING ACTIVITY

You will need these items for this activity:

• Chalkboard and chalk or marker board and markers

Before class, write the words of Acts 4:20 on the board. Also, write this sentence: "I'm going to Rome, and I'll take _____."

In class, say, *In today's study, Paul spoke to King Agrippa. Agrippa did not find that Paul broke any Roman laws. However, Paul already appealed his case to Caesar. So, Paul would go to Rome, the capital of the empire, to present his case there.*

Let's play a travel game. Think of something you would take with you if you planned to go to a big city like Rome. Each person will say, "I'm going to Rome, and I'll take a ____." You tell what you'll take. However, you need to listen carefully and remember what each person says that he or she will take.

When every person has had a turn, ask a volunteer to repeat what everyone said. For instance, the volunteer might say: "I'm going to Rome, and I'll take a ___. Mary's going to Rome, and she'll take a ___. John's going to Rome, and he'll take a _____."

Another version of the game presents more of a challenge. The first person says, "I'm going to Rome, and I'll take a ____." The second person says, "(first child's name) is going to Rome, and he'll take a ___. I'm going to Rome, and I'll take a ___." The third child repeats the names and objects of the first two people, and then states his name and object. The last child repeats everyone's name and all the objects. Say, *Wherever you go - to Rome or anywhere else - God goes with you. Wherever you go, God wants you to tell others about his love and about his Son, Jesus.* Read together Acts 4:20.

BIBLE LESSON

1. The trial before Felix (24:1-27)

After Paul had been in Caesarea for five days, the Jewish leaders finally arrived, with a lawyer. No doubt they had prepared their case with time. Read this chapter and answer the following:

1. What were the accusations that Tertullus, the lawyer, brought against Paul?
2. How did Paul respond to the accusations?
3. Surely Felix knew that Paul was innocent but didn't want problems with the Jewish leaders. On what pretext did the trial end?
4. What was the result of the private meeting between Felix and his wife, Drusilla, with Paul?

2. The trial before Festus (25:1-12)

In the last verse of chapter 24, we see that Paul stayed in prison for two years until Felix was replaced by Festus as governor. As soon as Festus arrived on the scene, the Jewish leaders urged him to do something with Paul.

* Read these verses and answer the questions:

1. Why do you think the Jewish leaders were still anxious to kill Paul, after two years?
2. Why didn't Paul want to go to Jerusalem for his trial?
3. Verses 11 and 12 are another example of God's plan at work. Read 23:11 again. How is God's plan being developed?

3. Festus goes higher (25:13-27)

A few days later, King Agrippa arrived in Caesarea. Festus, obviously not knowing what to do about Paul, decided to discuss the case with Agrippa.

* Read these verses and answer the following:

1. Why do you think the Roman authorities had so many problems deciding what to do with Paul?
2. Do you think that Festus accurately summarized Paul's case to King Agrippa?
3. Why did Festus take Paul before Agrippa?

4. The trial before Agrippa (26:1-32)

Again Paul is asked to respond to the accusations against him, this time before King Agrippa.

* Read the verses and answer the questions:

1. Why did Festus interrupt Paul?
2. Do you think there was an opportunity for Paul to convince Agrippa to be a Christian?
3. Agrippa told Festus, "This man could be set free if he had not appealed to the emperor" (v. 32).

Some scholars believe that Paul made a mistake in making that appeal. What do you think?

SUGGESTED ACTIVITIES

- Continue with the glossary of Words of our Faith.
- Add to the list the characters, places and objects that appear in this lesson.
- Do the games related to this lesson: Tell me the Person, Breaking News.

QUESTIONS

Acts 24, 25, 26

1. What did Tertullus beg Felix? (24:4)
That he would be kind enough to briefly hear them.

2. According to Tertullus, who was the ringleader of the Nazarene sect? (24:5)
Paul

3. According to Acts 24:6, what did Paul try to desecrate?
The temple

4. According to Acts 25:2, who presented their accusations against Paul?
The chief priests and Jewish leaders

5. What had Paul done against the Jewish law? (25:8)
Nothing wrong

6. Who gave Paul permission to defend himself? (26:1)
Agrippa

7. According to Acts 26:27, what was Paul aware of?
That Agrippa believed in the prophets.

FAITH IN THE MIDST OF THE STORM

Lesson 20

BIBLICAL PASSAGE: Acts 27 – 28:1

KEY VERSE: "Last night an angel of the God to whom I belong and whom I serve stood beside me and said, 'Do not be afraid, Paul.'" (Acts 27:23-24a)

TEACHING OBJECTIVES - To help the children:

1. God wants us to put our hope in him.

2. Understand that the hero of this story is God.

BIBLICAL COMMENTARY

The story of Paul's sea voyage to Rome is similar to many others in Greek literature. It is the result of obedience and submission, the opposite of the Old Testament journey of Jonah. Jonah's disobedience threatened the lives of everyone on the ship. Paul's obedience saved the lives of his shipmates.

Natural forces, beyond the control of the sailors, damaged the ship. There was no navigational guidance from the stars and sun, because they were blocked out by the storm. The skilled sailors tried at least four methods to salvage the ship. First, they secured the lifeboat. Second, they ran ropes under the ship to hold it together. Then, they lowered the anchor. Finally, they threw some cargo overboard. Despite these measures, the storm continued to beat the ship. The sailors lost hope.

Paul encouraged his fellow shipmates by sharing the angel's message that none of them would be lost. He demonstrated great faith when he proclaimed to the crew the angel's prophesy. Paul brought encouragement to his shipmates during the fury of the storm. It is encouraging to know that God is able to bring peace to us when we experience chaos in life.

WORDS OF OUR FAITH

An angel — a supernatural messenger from God.

OPENING ACTIVITY

You will need these items for this activity:

- An adult to tell the story of the shipwreck in a dramatic way
- Some tape on the floor to make the outline of a large ship
- A source of water to sprinkle on the children during the storm
- A fan to create some wind

Before class, use tape on the floor to make the outline of a large ship. Make it large enough for the whole class to sit inside. Ask an adult to tell the story of the shipwreck in a dramatic way. Ask a helper to be ready to start a fan to create the wind in the storm. Ask the helper to sprinkle water in the air to simulate the rain.

In class, say: *I invite you to take a ride in my ship, and here is our captain.* Introduce the volunteer. He or she then asks all the children to come on board the ship. They then retell the story of Paul and the shipwreck. The helper will turn on the fan and sprinkle the water at the appropriate point in the story.

After the story, thank the volunteer. Say, *God wanted Paul to go to Rome. God gave hope to Paul during the storm. Paul then gave hope to the other sailors did everything they could to save the ship and themselves — except to ask God for help. Paul helped the sailors know the one who is the true source of hope. God saved Paul's life and the life of everyone on the ship. God still brings hope to people today in the middle of difficult situations.*

BIBLE LESSON

1. Paul leaves for Rome (27:1-12)

Finally, the trip to take Paul to Rome was ready. He, along with the other prisoners, was in the charge of a Roman soldier named Julius. The trip was full of problems from the beginning because they left well into the year, with winter almost starting. As you read, keep in mind that these events occurred almost 2 thousand years ago, before any modern navigation equipment and without forecasting equipment. The group was traveling in a wooden boat, guided by the stars and pushed by the wind.

* Read these verses and answer the following:

1. What does verse 3 tell us about the Roman commander Julius?
2. It is interesting that Paul was probably the most experienced traveler on that ship. Do you think that his warning in verse 10 was the result of divine direction or human knowledge?

2. A traumatic trip (27:13–28:10)

From Fair Havens, where they had arrived and where Paul urged them to spend the winter, the ship left for another port on the same island of Crete. However, a storm took them out to sea. Luke describes the following events as an eyewitness (note that as a narrator he now uses the "we").

* Read the passage and answer the questions:

1. When the situation became very serious and the passengers lost all hope of being saved (v. 20), Paul began to take control of the ship's operations. In verse 21, the apostle reminds them that they would not be in that situation if they had listened to his advice in Fair Havens. Why do you think he did it?
2. Look at Paul's phrase in verse 23: "to whom I belong and whom I serve." What does this tell us about Paul?
3. Why do you think the Roman soldiers followed Paul's commands in verse 31?
4. In verses 42-43, we read that Julius saved the lives of the prisoners to save Paul's. Why would he do that?
5. How is Paul's stay on the island of Malta similar to his previous missionary trips?

SUGGESTED ACTIVITIES

- Continue with the glossary of Words of our faith. Add to the list the characters, places and objects that appear in this lesson.
- Choose and play games related to this lesson: Tell me the Person, Biblical Geography, Chest of Memories, Bible Bingo, Explosions, The Shipwreck, Answer and Draw, Charades, Drama, Breaking News.

QUESTIONS

Acts 27 – 28:1

1. Who belonged to the imperial battalion? (27:1)
A centurion named Julius.

2. What did Julius allow with great kindness in Sidon? (27:3)
He allowed Paul to visit his friends to they could provide for his needs.

3. Where was the Alexandria ship going? (27:6)
To Italy

4. According to Acts 27:12, where did they want to spend the winter?
In Phoenix

5. With what did they tie the ship's hull to reinforce it? (27:17)
With ropes

6. Why did Paul and the other crew members lose all hope of salvation? (27:20)
Neither sun nor stars appeared for many days and the storm continued raging.

7. How many nights had they drifted across the Adriatic Sea? (27:27)
Fourteen

8. What happened after Paul took the bread, gave thanks to God, broke it, and began to eat? (27:35)
They were encouraged and ate some food themselves.

9. How many people were on the boat? (27:37)
Two hundred seventy-six

10. What fastened itself to Paul's hand? (28:3)
A viper driven out by the heat

11. Who was the main official on the island of Malta? (28:7)
Publius

12. Who did Paul heal? (28:8)
Publius' father

THE END IS THE BEGINNING
Lesson 21

BIBLICAL PASSAGE: Acts 28:11-31

KEY VERSE: Last night an angel of the God to whom I belong and whom I serve stood beside me and said, "Do not be afraid, Paul."

TEACHING OBJECTIVES - To help the children:

1. God establishes and cares for his church through faithful believers.

2. We are all called to be witnesses of God, just as Paul was.

BIBLICAL COMMENTARY

When Paul finally reached Rome, he continued his mission of preaching the story of Jesus. Paul shared the account of his arrest and trial as the introduction of his testimony to the Jewish leaders. Like every other time he spoke to a Jewish audience, the reaction to Paul's message was mixed.

Paul quoted from Isaiah as he explained his experiences of sharing God's story with the Jewish people. Referring to Isaiah 6:9-10, Paul reiterated God's warning to the Jews. Paul reassured them that God would heal them if they chose humbly to receive the invitation to see, hear, understand, and obey God.

Paul probably experienced grief, knowing that his people did not accept the message of salvation. However, he continued to trust and obey God. In fact, Acts ends with a summary of Paul continuing boldly to preach the message of Jesus in Rome.

Throughout the second half of Acts, we read of Jewish rejection and Gentile acceptance of the gospel. Luke does not communicate in his book that the mission to the Jews was a failure. Some Jews accepted God's message. The gospel is for everyone, both Jew and Gentile. There is hope that all will accept the message. Jesus is our hope. With the power of the Holy Spirit, we can boldly proclaim this message to the world.

OPENING ACTIVITY

You will need these items for this activity:

- A piece of candy or small cookie for each child

- Five pieces of paper

- A marker

Before class, buy or make a small piece of candy or a cookie for each child. Make two signs: on one piece of paper write JEWS and on the other GENTILES.

In class, divide the children into two groups: the Jews and the Gentiles. Ask a volunteer from each group to hold the sign that you made.

Say, *I have some candy (or some cookies). Should I give them to the Jews or to the Gentiles? Why?* Let the children respond. Say, *I will give one to all of you.*

Let the children eat the treat then say, *When Paul entered a new city, he always spoke to the Jews first about the Gospel. However, many of the Jews refused to believe in Jesus. So, Paul preached the gospel to the Gentiles. Paul realized God wanted everyone to be a part of his kingdom. God wants you to be a part of his kingdom also.*

Review the steps of salvation. Invite any children who are not Christians to respond to God's call of salvation today. Pray with any who accept the invitation.

Say, *Paul travelled from Jerusalem to many cities. Wherever he went, he preached about Jesus. He fulfilled Acts 1:8 to go to Judea, Samaria, and to the uttermost parts of the world. You can tell your story now wherever you go.*

BIBLE LESSON

1. Rome, the end! (28:11-31)

After more than two years in Roman custody in Palestine, and after an almost disastrous trip to the Mediterranean, Paul finally arrived in Rome. Acts ends with a description of the two years Paul spent in custody.

* Read these verses and answer the following:

1. Do you notice that verse 15 speaks of the "brothers and sisters there" (Rome)? You will remember that Paul wrote the Epistle to the Romans to the Christian congregation there before making this trip of which we have been reading. How do you think he felt when he encountered these "brothers and sisters"?

2. One of Paul's first actions in Rome was to call together the Jewish leaders of that city. Why do you think he did that? (Remember his custom in previous missionary trips.)

3. What was the result of Paul's preaching and teaching to the Jews (verses 24-25)? How was it similar to the responses he received from the Jews of the other cities he had visited?

4. Verses 16 and 30 allow us to see how Paul lived in Rome. Although he was allowed to live in his own home and receive visitors, he remained in custody (in what we would today call "house arrest"). How did Paul react to this situation?

5. The two years that Paul spent in Rome waiting for his trial were busy years. During that time, he wrote the Epistles to the Philippians, Colossians, Ephesians and Philemon. Read these references in some of those letters: Ephesians 6:19-22; Philippians 1:12-14; 4:18, 21-22; Colossians 4:7-10; Philemon 1-25. What do you think now about Paul's activities after reading these verses?

2. Farewell to Acts

Congratulations! You have finished reading one of the most exciting books in the New Testament. But before you leave, take a few moments to reflect on what you have learned. Browse the pages of Acts. Take a break in some of your favorite passages. Go back to using this study guide and review some of the things you have written. Let God speak to you again through the book of the Acts. Take a few moments to answer these last questions:

1. The book of Acts ends abruptly, without telling us what happened to Paul. Remember that Luke's purpose in writing the book was not to tell us a biography of Paul (or anyone else). It was to tell us how the Church spread by fulfilling the promise of Jesus to the small group of disciples: "But you will receive power when the Holy Spirit comes on you; and you will be my witnesses in Jerusalem, and in all Judea and Samaria, and to the ends of the earth." (1: 8). How much of this purpose do you think Luke achieved?

2. Thinking about the history of the Church that Luke described to us (from a small group of Christians in Jerusalem led by Peter to the large number of congregations scattered throughout Asia Minor and Eastern Europe that Paul founded), the leadership of the Holy Spirit is clear and unmistakable. How would you describe his leadership?

3. What is the most important lesson you learned from the Book of Acts?

SUGGESTED ACTIVITIES

• Continue with the glossary of Words of our Faith. Add to the list the characters, places and objects that appear in this lesson.

• Do the games related to this lesson: Chest of Memories.

QUESTIONS
Acts 28:11-31

1. According to Acts 28:11, how long were they in Malta?
Three months

2. What was the last stop before arriving in Rome? (28:13-14)
Puteoli

3. What did Paul do from the law of Moses and the prophets from morning until evening? (28:23)
He tried to persuade them about Jesus

4. According to Acts 28:28, who will listen?
The Gentiles.

5. Who did Paul receive during the two full years that he stayed in the house he had rented? (28:30)
All who came to see him

ACTIVITIES FOR TEACHING MEMORY VERSES

BIBLE VERSE FUN

Ask the children to sit in a straight line. Tell the first child to stand, to say the first word of the verse, to wave both hands excitedly in the air, and to sit down. Ask the second child to stand, to say the second word of the verse, to wave both hands excitedly in the air, and to sit down.

Continue until the verse is complete. If a child forgets a word or says the wrong word, let the other children tell the correct word. Encourage the children to say the verse quickly so that their motions look like an ocean wave.

BIBLE PASS

You will need a Bible and a source of music for this activity.

Have the children sit in a circle. Give one child the Bible. When the music starts, tell the children to pass the Bible around the circle.

When the music stops, the child holding the Bible says the Bible verse. Tactfully stop the music so each child has an opportunity to say the verse.

BIBLE VERSE RACE

Write each word or phrase of a Bible verse on a piece of paper. Make two sets, one for each team.

Divide the class into two teams. Place a set of word cards on the floor in front of each team. Scramble the order of the cards. After a signal, let the first child on each team find the first word of the verse and run to a goal line.

The child places the card on the floor and races back to the second player. That child picks up the second word of the verse and races with it to the goal line. Continue until one team completes the verse in perfect order. Allow time for the second team to complete its verse. Then have both teams recite the verse together.

BIBLE VERSE LINE UP

Write each word or phrase of a Bible verse on a piece of paper.

Give each child a verse card. Instruct the children with cards to go to different parts of the room and hold up the card. Choose another child to line up the children in the correct order of the verse. Then have the class read the verse together.

HIDE AND SEEK MEMORY GAME

Prepare papers and hide them in advance for this activity.

Write each word of the memory verse on a separate piece of paper. Hide the individual words around the room. Ask the children to find the words and to arrange them in the correct order. Recite the memory verse.

STAND UP VERSES

Instruct the children to sit in a circle. Instruct the first child to stand and say the first word of the verse, and then he or she sits down. The second child stands and says the second word of the verse, and then he or she sits down. Continue until the children complete the verse. Encourage the children to play again, but to go faster than the previous time. Let the children see how quickly they can say the verse.

MISSING WORDS MEMORY GAME

You will need a chalkboard, marker board, or paper for this activity.

Write the memory verse on a chalkboard or marker board. Ask the children to recite the verse. Permit a child to erase one word, and then ask the children to repeat the verse (including the missing word.) Continue until all the words disappear, and the children say the verse from memory. If a chalkboard or marker board is not available, write each word of the verse on a separate piece of paper, and ask the children to remove one word at a time.

MEMORY VERSES

But you will receive power when the Holy Spirit comes on you; and you will be my witnesses in Jerusalem, and in all Judea and Samaria, and to the ends of the earth.	Acts 1:8
They devoted themselves to the apostles' teaching and to fellowship, to the breaking of bread and to prayer.	Acts 2:42
They sold property and possessions to give to anyone who had need.	Acts 2:45
Then Peter said, "Silver or gold I do not have, but what I do have I give you. In the name of Jesus Christ of Nazareth, walk."	Acts 3:6
Salvation is found in no one else, for there is no other name under heaven given to mankind by which we must be saved.	Acts 4:12
All the believers were one in heart and mind. No one claimed that any of their possessions was their own, but they shared everything they had.	Acts 4:32
So the word of God spread. The number of disciples in Jerusalem increased rapidly, and a large number of priests became obedient to the faith.	Acts 6:7
Those who had been scattered preached the word wherever they went. Philip went down to a city in Samaria and proclaimed the Messiah there.	Acts 8:4-5
But the Lord said to Ananias, "Go! This man is my chosen instrument to proclaim my name to the Gentiles and their kings and to the people of Israel."	Acts 9:15
He and all his family were devout and God-fearing; he gave generously to those in need and prayed to God regularly.	Acts 10:2
Then Peter began to speak: "I now realize how true it is that God does not show favoritism."	Acts 10:34
Then Peter came to himself and said, "Now I know without a doubt that the Lord has sent his angel and rescued me from Herod's clutches and from everything the Jewish people were hoping would happen."	Acts 12:11

Strengthening the disciples and encouraging them to remain true to the faith. "We must go through many hardships to enter the kingdom of God," they said.	Acts 14:22
God, who knows the heart, showed that he accepted them by giving the Holy Spirit to them, just as he did to us.	Acts 15:8
They replied, "Believe in the Lord Jesus, and you will be saved—you and your household."	Acts 16:31
The God who made the world and everything in it is the Lord of heaven and earth and does not live in temples built by human hands.	Acts 17:24
In this way the word of the Lord spread widely and grew in power.	Acts 19:20
However, I consider my life worth nothing to me; my only aim is to finish the race and complete the task the Lord Jesus has given me—the task of testifying to the good news of God's grace.	Acts 20:24
You will be his witness to all people of what you have seen and heard.	Acts 22:15
The following night the Lord stood near Paul and said, "Take courage! As you have testified about me in Jerusalem, so you must also testify in Rome."	Acts 23:11
So I strive always to keep my conscience clear before God and man.	Acts 24:16
Last night an angel of the God to whom I belong and whom I serve stood beside me and said, "Do not be afraid, Paul."	Acts 27:23-24a

CERTIFICATE OF COMPLETION

Presented to:

NAME

Congratulations for having successfully
completed the Bible Studies for Children: ACTS

Date: _____

Teacher _____

AWARD OF EXCELLENCE

Presented to:

Well done! We recognize your outstanding achievement in the Bible Study for Children: ACTS

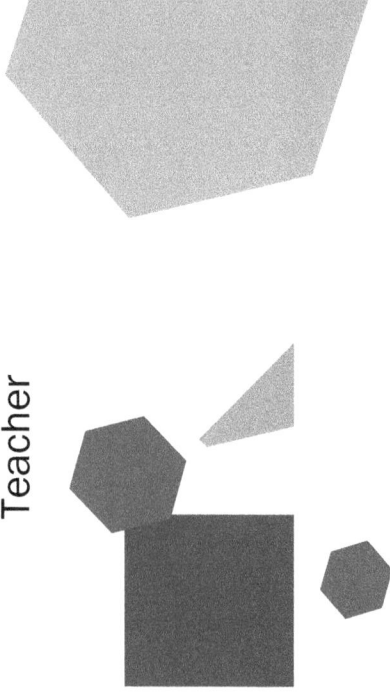

Teacher

Place:

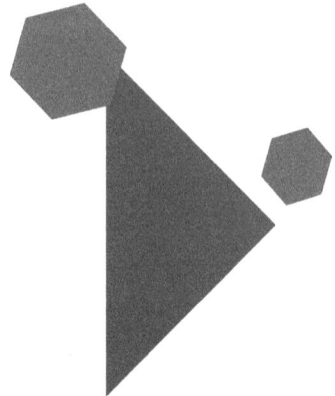

GUIDE FOR CHILDREN'S BIBLE QUIZZING USING GAMES AND ACTIVITIES

WHAT IS CHILDREN'S BIBLE QUIZZING MINISTRY?

Mission	Vision	Values
of Jesus by studying and asuring God's Word in the hearts.	evangelism and a dynamic tool of discipleship	Tolerance Working as a team

Based on a principle of learning by playing, the Children's Bible Quizzing Ministry or CBQM its initials, is part of the Discipleship Ministries tools for the task of discipleship in local churches. We invite you to get to know the dynamic and attractive approach of this ministry which allows children to get actively involved, learn, and treasure with greater strength and depth the biblical content studied.

We firmly believe that "instructing the child in the way he should go" (Proverbs 22:6) is a pressing mandate that the Lord gives us, especially in our confused societies in which our children are easily dying - literally and spiritually. We trust that according to this experiential teaching of CBQM, the children "will not leave the right path" even when they leave their childhood behind.

WHAT IS THE ORGANIZATION OF CBQM?

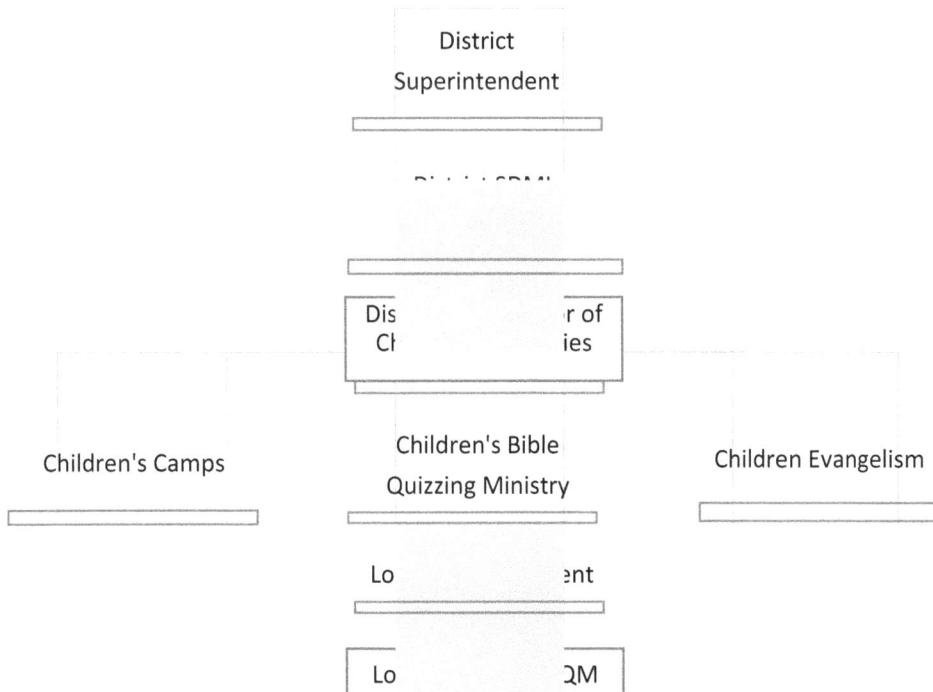

District Superintendent

Dis... r of Cl... ies

Children's Camps   Children's Bible Quizzing Ministry   Children Evangelism

Lo... nt

Lo... QM

WHAT RESOURCES ARE AVAILABLE FOR CBQM - GAMES AND ACTIVITIES?

The Bible, is the most important resource. Please take into account the version. We will be using the New International Version because its language is simple and facilitates the children's understanding. It will be used for reading, memory verses, specific words, etc.	You can also visit the Mesoamerica Region Discipleship Ministries Page where you will find this and other resources to work with children and for other church ministries. www.SdmiResources.MesoamericaRegion.org	The Coaches Guide of Bible Studies, Games and Activities, and Questions and Answers is a book that contains lessons from the study book, in this case Acts. It gives you ideas for developing lessons for children, learning dynamics, tools to memorize verses, and questions for basic and advanced competition levels.
	Maps – These maps will facilitate the teaching – learning process, allowing children to better understand events.	

HOW DO I FORM A TEAM IN MY LOCAL CHURCH?

The local SDMI president must get the materials that are available for CBQM (physical copy or download electronic copies), select a brother / sister who is helpful, dynamic and who loves working with children to work as a team coach.	**Coach** - his/her function is to prepare the team, motivating them to study the Word, giving or coordinating the Bible lessons, leading the learning activities and games, accompanying the team to all the quiz demonstrations organized by the district, etc.	**Team** – the team will consist of a maximum of 10 children from 7 to 11 years of age. (They may be younger, but they should be able to read and write.)

HOW DO WE PREPARE THE CHILDREN?

A teaching and study time must be established with the team. The study must consider the theme assigned for the bible quizzing.

To study the subject better, it can be divided into chapters or specific events, for this use the coach's guide which will guide you in this process. Start with teaching about the events, and discuss with them by using questions and having them answer from memory about situations, characters, places and names. Explain facts that motivate the curiosity of the team in terms of customs, meaning of objects or rites and other interesting features that complement and clarify the text and context read. Create lists of words, names, places, objects, animals. Find out in which other books of the Bible the main characters are mentioned. Have the children memorize the key verses exactly. Help the children memorize events and sequences of the stories, in a non-textual way, so they can relate it as completely as possible. It is necessary to help them remember important data. Guide them to discover individually and as a team the teaching of God for their lives and perform the games that are related to the lesson studied.

THIS STUDY GUIDE CAN HELP WITH THE FOLLOWING THEMES:

- Where did this character(s) come from?
- Who are they related to?
- Where does the story unfold?
- How does God work in their lives?
- What is the reason why this story is found in the Bible?
- How does this passage relate to Christ and therefore to salvation?
- Take each story and bring it to the current time. How would you do it?
- What values are found in the story?
- What places are mentioned? Find them on a map.
- What are the characters like?
- What characteristics do they have?
- What things stand out in the culture and do you need to investigate (animals, crafts, rites or customs)?

63

IN ADDITION:

- Invite Sunday School teachers and / or people with theological studies to teach lessons about the topic and answer questions.
- Encourage people of the church to support the team.
- Practice each game only after having studied and clarified the subject considerably.
- Remember that it is important to establish the skills in which the child performs best.

EACH TEAM MUST PREPARE:

- A name for the team, which should be based on the theme of the study. It must be presented in a creative way and will have a value of 10 points.
- A badge - something that identifies the team, such as a shirt, a hat, a uniform, etc. The presentation of your badge and the badge as such will have a value of 10 points.
- A mascot, which preferably should be an animal that is related to the theme of the study and that is contained in a biblical teaching. The costume must be creative, and the presentation of the mascot has a value of 20 points.
- A team cheer. This should be based on the subject of study and the name of the team, must not contain words or offensive ideas to other teams, its maximum duration is 1 minute, and its creative presentation will have a value of 20 points.

ANNUAL STUDY CYCLE

- ACTS - 2019
- GENESIS - 2020
- EXODUS - 2021
- JOSHUA, JUDGES & RUTH - 2022
- 1 & 2 SAMUEL – 2023
- MATTHEW – 2024

DEMONSTRATION OFFICIALS

Moderator – He or she must be an impartial person. They can be a guest from another district or from a local church that is not participating in the demonstration. • This is the person who chooses the games and prepares the material for them. • Directs the competition. • Reads the instructions for each category or game. • Chooses the team of judges.	**Judges** - They must be impartial. They can be invited from another district or from a church that is not participating. A judge will be assigned to each participating team. That is, if there are 5 teams participating, there must be 5 judges. They must: • Ensure that the rules of each game are kept. • Oversee the participant(s) from that team during each game. • Let the moderator know if any rules are broken.	**Time Judge** – They must keep time for each game, giving the signal for the start and the end of the time allotted for the game.

NOTES

If you have worked with CBQM before, you will notice some changes. For example, we have changed the word "trainer" to "coach" because we think it is more appropriate.

Some games have been modified, others have been removed and new games directly related to the subject of study have been added.

Remember that a competition is a demonstration, because each team demonstrates how much they have learned from the Word of God. We must ensure that competitiveness is healthy and creates bonds of friendship between the participating teams.

In some games the assumption is made of a demonstration between two or three teams, these are only examples for a better understanding of the game.

MEMORIZATION CATEGORY

Memorization and reasoning are fundamental for learning, and repetition is one of the keys to memorization. The objective of this category is to help children memorize and understand the Bible in a dynamic and attractive way.

SOME MEMORIZATION TECHNIQUES:
- Connect and link
- Associate objects with places
- Create stories
- Link words with numbers to remember sequences
- Draw mental maps
- Acronyms, using the first letter of each word
- Repeat the keywords
- Use all the senses

For a local, district, zone, national demonstration, etc. the moderator will choose:

3 Memorization Games

The teams will know which specific games will be played ONLY on the day of the demonstration.

WORD WEAPON (NEW GAME)

INSTRUCTIONS:

1. The moderator gives each team a sheet with a list of 10 consonants to play; each team has the freedom to choose 3 vowels which must be written on the same sheet.
2. When given the start signal, the participants from the team should think of the largest number of words with the list of letters they have. They can use a letter more than once in a word. All words must be related to the subject of study and have at least 4 letters.
3. At the end of time, the judge reviews and counts their words, giving them 5 points for each correct word.

CONSULTATIONS:

Consultation is allowed only between the 3 PARTICIPANTS of each team.

FOUL:

If the participants consult with the coach or with the other children of the team, the judge will indicate it and the value of a word is deducted.

If someone in the audience says a word out loud, the value of a word is deducted from each team.

EXAMPLE:

POINTS
5 points for each correct word

TIME
2 minutes

PARTICIPANTS
3 per team

MODE
Simultaneous - all teams participate at one time

MATERIALS
• One piece of paper, with the consonants to be used for the game, for each team.   • A pen for each team

---

CONSONANTS TO PLAY:
C D F J L P R S T H

THE CHILDREN OF TEAM PAUL CHOOSE THE FOLLOWING VOWELS:
A E O

Peter	Dorcas
Father	Heal
Joseph	Share
Herod	
Sorcerer	
Lord	

The participants of the Team Paul made a list of 9 words, the judge reviewed them and they all were correct, for which they scored 45 points for their team.

ADVANCE (NEW GAME)

INSTRUCTIONS:

1. The moderator draws the order in which the teams participate and they are placed in front of their three rings (hula hoops).

2. The first participant must say a verse from the list of memory verses (their choice). They must say it exactly; if it is correct, the moderator indicates it and the participant advances into the first ring.

3. The next participant must recite another verse (their choice); the difficulty is that they cannot recite a verse that has already been quoted by another participant; in case this happens, the child will not be able to advance.

If during the first 30 seconds the child does not begin to say his verse, he loses the opportunity and does not advance.

10 points are awarded for each verse correctly quoted, up to 30 points per team

CONSULTATIONS:
Not permitted.

FOUL:
If the audience says a part of the verse out loud or if the child consults with their coach or team, they are disqualified and their participation in this game is canceled.

SUGGESTION:
If there were many teams participating, the game can be reduced to 2 rings (verses) per team.

POINTS
10 points for each correct verse

TIME
30 seconds to start,
1 minute to finish

PARTICIPANTS
1 per team

MODE
One team at a time, alternating

MATERIALS
- Three hoops (hula hoops) per team.
- The judge must have the list of memory verses.

EXAMPLE:

Isabel of team "Paul" correctly recited a verse, gaining 10 points for her team.
John of the team "Missionaries for Jesus" recited a different verse, and gained 10 points for his team.
Camila of the team "Acts that transform" advanced 1 ring after she quoted a different verse and gained 10 points for her team.

Isabel of Team "Paul" advanced to the 2nd ring with her quote of another verse, and her team won 20 points.
John of team "Missionaries for Jesus", and Camila from "Acts that Transform" successfully quoted 3 verses in total, ending up in ring 3, gaining 30 points in total for their teams.

STOP

INSTRUCTIONS:

1. The moderator will give 1 answer sheet to each team with the following titles: LETTER; NAME OF PERSON; OBJECT, ANIMAL or PLANT; PLACE; and TOTAL. (See example below.)

2. The moderator starts the game by beginning to recite the alphabet in a loud voice, starting with the letter "A" and continues the alphabet in a low voice. A judge will say STOP! at a certain point, and the game with start with the letter that the moderator was saying when the judge said STOP! The moderator will say the first letter to be used for the game, and then begins the count of 2 minutes for the participants to answer.

3. The child who finishes his/her answer sheet first must say out loud, "STOP!" Then the other participants will no longer be able to fill in more answers.

4. Next, a second letter will be chosen, and the 2nd round begins. After playing the two suggested rounds, the children hand in their answer sheets. If there are correct words that are repeated on the answer sheets of other participants, those answers receive 5 points each. For the answers that are correct and not repeated, they receive 10 points each.

CONSULTATIONS:
Not permitted.

FOUL:
If A judge sees that a participant continues to fill out their ballot after another participant has said STOP, all answers are forfeited.

SUGGESTION:
Play two letters.

NAME: Lucas Álvarez					TEAM: Paul		
LETTER	NAME OF PERSON	points	OBJECT, ANIMAL OR PLANT	points	PLACE	points	TOTAL
P	Paul	10	Port	5	Paphos	10	25
M	Matthias	10	Man	10	Mysia	10	30
						FINAL TOTAL	55

NAME: Priscila Amaya					TEAM: Acts that transform		
LETTER	NAME OF PERSON	points	OBJECT, ANIMAL OR PLANT	points	PLACE	points	TOTAL
P	Priscilla	10	Port	5	Pamphylia	10	25
M	Mary	10	Mats	10	------	0	20
						FINAL TOTAL	45

THE DICE

INSTRUCTIONS:

The moderator prepares a dice on which actions will be written on each side: SING A SONG, SAY A VERSE, CHARACTERISTICS OF A BIBLE CHARACTER.

1. Each team draws a participation number. The moderator starts with number 1.

2. Number 1 participant is called forward, rolls the dice, and then has 30 seconds to do the activity that comes up on the top of the dice. If the participant is able to do the action, the judge gives 20 points to the team. If the participant doesn't do the action or remains silent during the 30 seconds, the judge will not award a score.

3. Next, the moderator will call up the next participant to roll the dice, and so forth until each team has participated.

CONSULTATIONS:

Not permitted.

FOUL:

If the boy or girl consults with his coach or team, or the audience helps them, the judge will indicate it and the moderator will give them another opportunity to throw the dice. If the same thing happens again, that person's participation in this game is canceled.

EXAMPLE OF A DICE:

POINTS
20 points

TIME
1 minute

PARTICIPANTS
1 per team

MODE
One team at a time

MATERIALS
• A large dice (follow the example below)

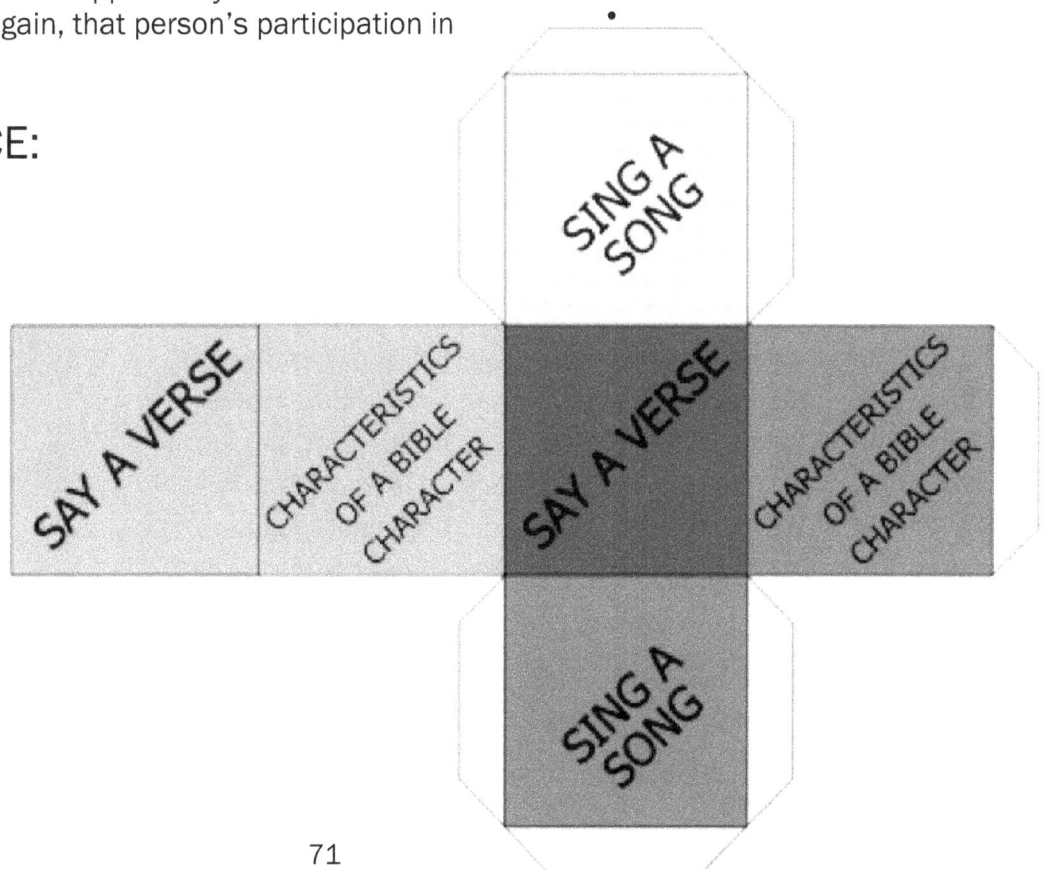

COMPLETE THE WORD

INSTRUCTIONS:

1. This game is based on the game "hangman" or "Wheel of Fortune." Provide as many spaces as there are letters in the word the participant has to discover. A sub-theme related to the word is specified. For example: Places, friendships, teachings, writings, family, objects, characteristics, etc.

2. The participant must say letters to complete the word. She/he has 5 seconds to give a letter. If she exceeds the time without saying a letter, that is considered an error. If she says a letter that is part of the word, it is placed in the blank space(s) as many times as it appears in the word. If the letter mentioned is not part of the word, it is considered an error and the letter is written to the side in view of the participant as an aid not to repeat it.

3. If, when filling in the blank spaces of the word, she discovers the hidden word, she can say it, and she has successful completed the game. If it is not correct, it is considered an error. The participant can make a maximum of 5 errors.

4. These errors are visualized with the picture that has been divided up into 5 pieces. Each time an error is made, another piece of the picture is added. If the participant does not discover the word before 5 errors are made, the picture is completed and the moderator says the word. The team does not get any points.

5. If the participant discovers the correct word before completing the picture, their team receives 10 points. If he doesn't discover the word, his team does not receive any point.

Then it is the next team's turn.

CONSULTATIONS:
Not permitted.

FOUL:

If the participant consults with another team member or anyone else, the judge will inform the moderator, and the moderator will cancel the word to complete, and start again with another word if this is the first offense. If the infraction is repeated, the participant is disqualified, and the team is no longer eligible to compete in this particular game.

SUGGESTION:
In a demonstration, it would be preferable to use a single category and that all words have the same number of letters.

POINTS
20 points

TIME
5 minutes

PARTICIPANTS
1 per team

MODE
One team as a time

MATERIALS

- Blackboard or poster board and markers
- Envelopes with the name of the category and the word to complete. One per team and some extras.
- A picture divided into 5 pieces (see example of the clown below)

EXAMPLE: The category is "PLACES" and the word to complete is "SALAMINA" so the participant starts with 8 spaces: _ _ _ _ _ _ _ _

The participant mentions the vowel "A" which is found in the word. The moderator proceeds to place the letter in each space in which it appears in the word.

_ A _ A _ _ _ A

The participant mentions the consonant "M" which is found in the word, for which the moderator proceeds to place the letter in each space where it appears in the word.

_ A _ A M _ _ A

The participant mentions the consonant "R" which is NOT found in the word, so the moderator proceeds to place the letter on the side of the word so that the participant does not repeat it; He also adds a piece of the picture to the board/paper.

_ A _ A M _ _ A   R

The game continues until the participant completes or correctly discovers the word (20 points for the team), or the picture is completed after 5 errors (game over – 0 points for the team).

Then it is the next team's turn.

Examples of Topics and Words:

PEOPLE					
1	2	3	4	5	6
P	E	T	E	R	
P	A	U	L		
L	Y	D	I	A	
A	E	N	E	A	S
S	I	L	A	S	
E	L	Y	M	A	S
P	H	I	L	I	P
D	O	R	C	A	S
A	Q	U	I	L	A
G	A	L	L	I	O
M	A	R	K		

PLACES							
1	2	3	4	5	6	7	8
C	A	E	S	A	R	E	A
P	H	I	L	I	P	P	I
D	A	M	A	S	C	U	S
G	A	L	A	T	I	A	
B	I	T	H	Y	N	I	A
C	O	R	I	N	T	H	
P	E	R	G	A	M	O	N
C	I	L	I	C	I	A	
N	E	A	P	O	L	I	S
P	A	P	H	O	S		
S	E	L	E	U	C	I	A

OBJECTS OR ANIMALS						
1	2	3	4	5	6	7
A	N	C	H	O	R	
B	O	A	T			
C	L	O	U	D		
B	R	E	A	D		
B	U	L	L	S		
C	L	O	T	H		
S	I	L	V	E	R	
S	H	O	P	S		
W	I	N	D	O	W	
C	H	A	I	N	S	
C	O	I	N	S		

CROSSWORD PUZZLE

INSTRUCTIONS:

1. Each team is given a crossword puzzle of 6 or 8 questions. Each team is given five minutes to answer. Teams must submit their crossword puzzle in the allotted time.
2. At the end of the five minutes, 10 points are awarded for each correct answer.

CONSULTATIONS:

Consultation is only allowed among the 3 participants of the team.

FOUL:

If team members consult with the coach or other children of the team who are not participating, the judge will inform the moderator and the moderator will disqualify the crossword of that team, thereby eliminating their participation in this game only.

EXAMPLE 1:

Based on "Peter's miraculous escape from jail" (Acts 12:1-19)

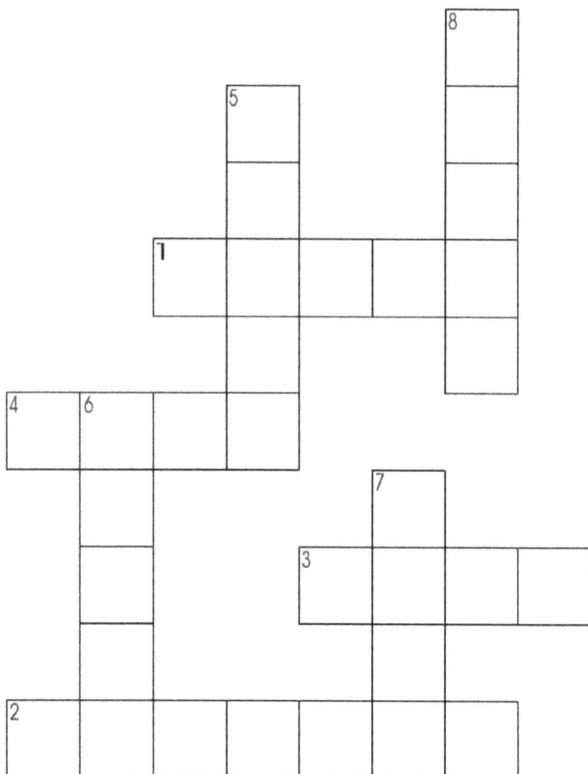

Horizontal:

1. Who commanded the arrest of Peter? **Herod**
2. What did the Angel tell Peter to put on? **Clothes**
3. What was the nickname of Mary's son John? **Mark**
4. With what did Peter make signs that they should be silent? **Hand**

Vertical:

5. At what party did Herod order Peter to be arrested? **Bread**
6. Who appeared to Peter in the cell? **Angel**
7. What opened by itself? **Gate**
8. What was the name of the servant who recognized Peter's voice? **Rhoda**

EXAMPLE 2:

Based on "Jesus taken to heaven" Acts 1:1-11

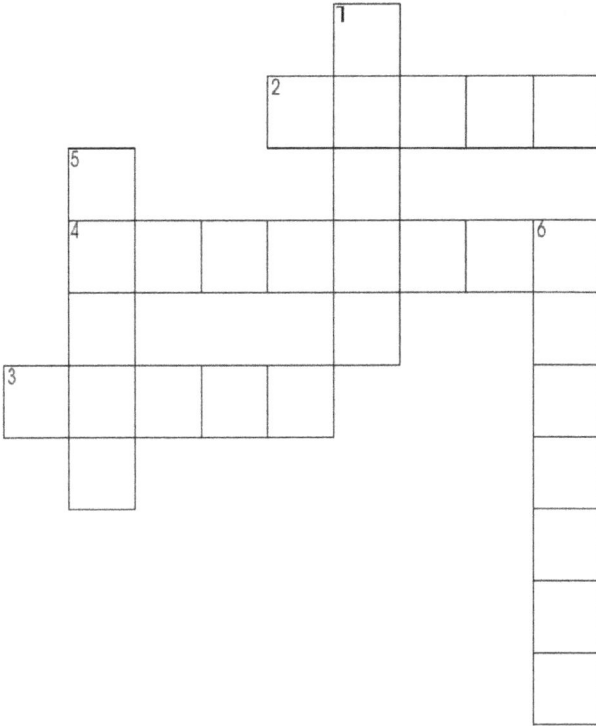

Across

2. What would they receive when the Holy Spirit arrived? **POWER**

3. Who will come again? **JESUS**

4. To whom did he give instructions by means of the Holy Spirit? **APOSTLES**

Down

1. For how many days did Jesus appear to them and tell them about the kingdom of God? **FORTY**

5. With what did John baptize? **WATER**

6. One of the places where they would be witnesses? **SAMARIA**

EXAMPLE 3:

Based on "The conversion of Saul" Acts 9:1-19

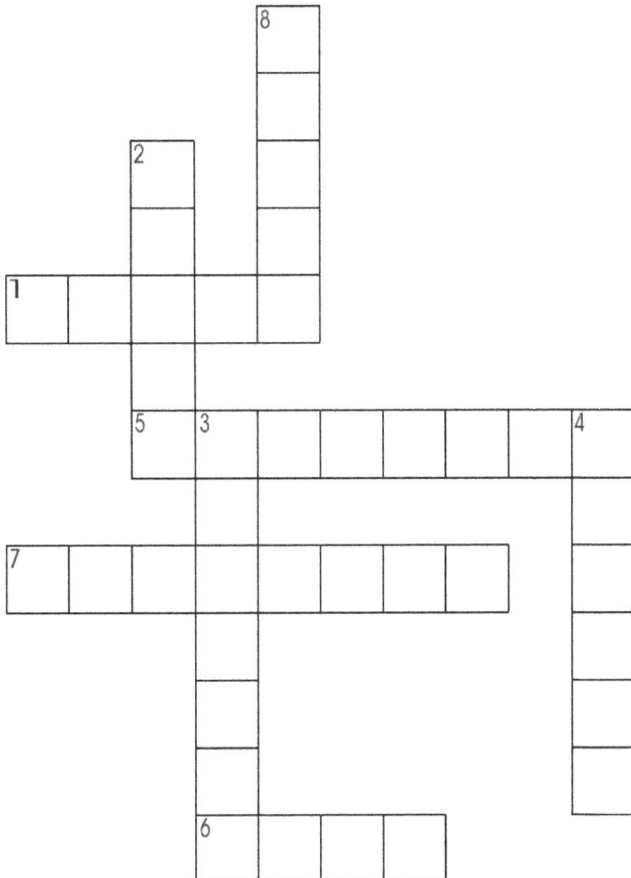

Across

1. What did Saul hear? **VOICE**

5. Where was Saul going? **DAMASCUS**

6. Who fell to the ground? **SAUL**

7. What was the name of the street where the house of Judas was? **STRAIGHT**

Down

2. What happened to Saul? He became what? **BLIND**

3. Who did the Lord call in a vision? **ANANIAS**

4. What was similar to what fell from Saul's eyes? **SCALES**

8. How many days was Saul blind? **THREE**

TELL ME THE PERSON

INSTRUCTIONS:

This is a guessing game which is based on people from the book being studied; Each riddle must have three to four clues about a character in the book to be studied.

1. The moderator must have two questions for each participating team.
2. Each participant must answer their question without consulting with his/her teammate. The participant has one minute to give the answer. If the answer is correct, the moderator says "**CORRECT**" and the judges award 20 points to the team (for each correct answer). If the answer is not correct or is not answered in the given time, the participant loses their chance and the moderator gives the correct answer. (No points are awarded to the team.)
3. The moderator continues with a participant from the other team, and alternates between each of the teams until each of the 2 participants from each team have been given the opportunity to answer a question.

CONSULTATIONS:

Not permitted.

FOUL:

If a judge observes that a participant consults with his/her team or someone else present, the moderator will cancel the question and ask a different question. If the participant has already been caught doing this before, the moderator will cancel the question and the team loses its opportunity.

POINTS
20 points for each correct answer

TIME
1 minute

PARTICIPANTS
2 per team

MODE
One team at a time, alternating

MATERIALS
• Envelopes with the clues, two per team and some extras.

EXAMPLES OF RIDDLES:

I joined a lot with John, they sent me to the Samaritans to pray for them so that they would receive the Holy Spirit, I was criticized by those who defended the circumcision, and I miraculously escaped from prison. Who am I? **Peter**	I was blind for three days. I traveled to many places with Barnabas. One of my disciples was named Timothy. I was with Silas in jail. Who I am? **Paul**	I live in Lydda. I was a paralytic and stuck in bed for eight years. One day Peter told me "Jesus Christ heals you. Get up and roll up your mat." Who am I? **Aeneas (Acts 9)**
I live in Caesarea and I am known as the Italian, my family and I are devotees and God fearing, I paid tribute to Peter but he told me not to do it. Who I am? **Cornelius (Acts 10)**	I like to worship God, I am from the city of Thyatira and I sell purple fabric, I hosted Paul and his disciples in my house. Who am I? **(Lydia) (Acts 16)**	We are of very noble character, every day we examine the Word, we sent Paul to the coast when the Jews came to make a fuss. Who are we? **The Bereans (Acts 17)**
We dedicate ourselves to making tents. We accompanied Paul on his trip to Syria. We instructed Apollo on the path of God. Who are we? **Aquila & Priscilla (Acts 18)**	I get good income from my trade. I make shrines to Artemis. I gathered other craftsmen to oppose Paul. Who I am? **Demetrius the Silversmith (Acts 19)**	I was sitting in a window listening to Paul's speech that lasted until dawn, I fell asleep and fell from the third floor. Who I am? **Eutychus (Acts 20)**
With my wife Drusilla we sent for Paul and we heard him speak about his faith in Christ Jesus. My successor was Porcius Festus, but because he wanted to please the Jews, he imprisoned Paul. Who I am? **Felix (Acts 24)**	We entered the courtroom with all pomp, accompanied by high-ranking officials and important people of the city. I concluded that Paul did not deserve death and send him to Rome. Who I am? **King Agrippa (Acts 25)**	Several prisoners, including Paul, were handed over to me. We sailed through a great storm. When the ship wrecked, the soldiers wanted to kill the prisoners, but I prevented it to save Paul's life. Who am I? **Julius The Centurion (Acts 27)**

WHERE WAS PAUL? (NEW GAME)

INSTRUCTIONS:

Each participant is presented with an answer sheet containing two columns. In a column are written three questions of places where Paul was, and in the other column, the names of the places. The participants must draw an arrow from the question to the correct place.

1. The moderator gives a pencil and an answer sheet (the same answer sheet for everyone) to each participant which will be placed face down.

2. When the start signal is given, the participants will all turn over their answer sheets and start the game at the same time and join the boxes with arrows.

3. When they are finished or at the end of the allotted time, the answer sheets are given to the judges. For each correct answer, they score 10 points for their team.

CONSULTATIONS:

Not permitted.

FOUL:

If a judge observes one of the participants trying to see the answers of another participant, the ballot is withdrawn and that person's participation in this game is ended.

EXAMPLES:

	POINTS
	10 points for each correct answer

	TIME
	3 minutes

	PARTICIPANTS
	1 per team

	MODE
	Simultaneous - all teams participate at one time

	MATERIALS
	• One answer sheet per team • A pencil per team

Where Paul and Barnabas were when they answered b: "We had to speak the word of God to you first. Since you reject it and do not consider yourselves worthy of eternal life, we now turn to the Gentiles."

Where was Paul when he met Lydia the purple cloth vendor and stayed at her house?

Where was Paul when he began to pray and sing hymns to God along with Silas, and suddenly there was an earthquake?

IN JAIL
(Acts 16)

PISIDIAN ANTIOCH
(Acts 13)

PHILIPPI
(Acts 16)

Where Paul was when they met a sorcerer, a false Jewish prophet named Bar-Jesus.	**ISLAND OF PAPHOS** (Acts 13)
The people of the city were divided: some sided with the Jews, and others with the apostles.	**IN ICONIUM** (Acts 14)
Where Paul was when the Lord told him in a vision "Do not be afraid; keep on speaking, do not be silent. For I am with you … "	**IN CORINTH** (Acts 18)

Where was Paul when he told a man crippled from birth, "Stand up on your feet!" The man jumped and started walking.	**THESSALONICA** (Acts 17)
Where Paul was when he said to the Jews in the synagogue: "This Jesus I am proclaiming to you is the Messiah."	**ATHENS** (Acts 17)
Where Paul was when he announced the good news of Jesus and the resurrection, and then they took him to a meeting of the Areopagus.	**IN LYSTRA** (Acts 14)

BIBLICAL GEOGRAPHY

INSTRUCTIONS:
1. Each team is provided with a map.
2. The Bible passage is read and the team should mark the places mentioned in the reading. The reading is not repeated, nor are questions or interruptions accepted. Participants on the same team can consult each other in a low voice.
3. At the end of the reading, the judges review the maps. 5 points are awarded for each map location correctly marked.

CONSULTATIONS:
The 3 participants of the same team can consult with one another in low voices.

FOUL:
The interruption of the reading with questions or requests, getting out of your place, consulting with each other in loud voices, or consulting with anyone other than the 3 participants is considered a foul. If a foul occurs, the judge will inform the moderator to draw attention to the problem at once. If it is repeated on a second occasion, the game is paused and the team is disqualified from the game. Then the rest of the participating teams will continue with the game.

SUGGESTED READINGS:
Acts 13:4-14
Acts 16:1-12
Acts 27:3-12

POINTS
5 points for each correct name

TIME
The time of the reading

PARTICIPANTS
3 per team

MODE
Simultaneous - all teams participate at one time

MATERIALS
• A map suitable for the reading • A marker or pen per team • A previously selected biblical passage

NOTE
In preparing for this game, make a large map to train your team. You can stick blown-up balloons in the places where important events happened. For example, Sergius Paulus became proconsul in Paphos, Paul spoke at the Areopagus in Athens, and Paul gives life back to Eutychus in Troas.

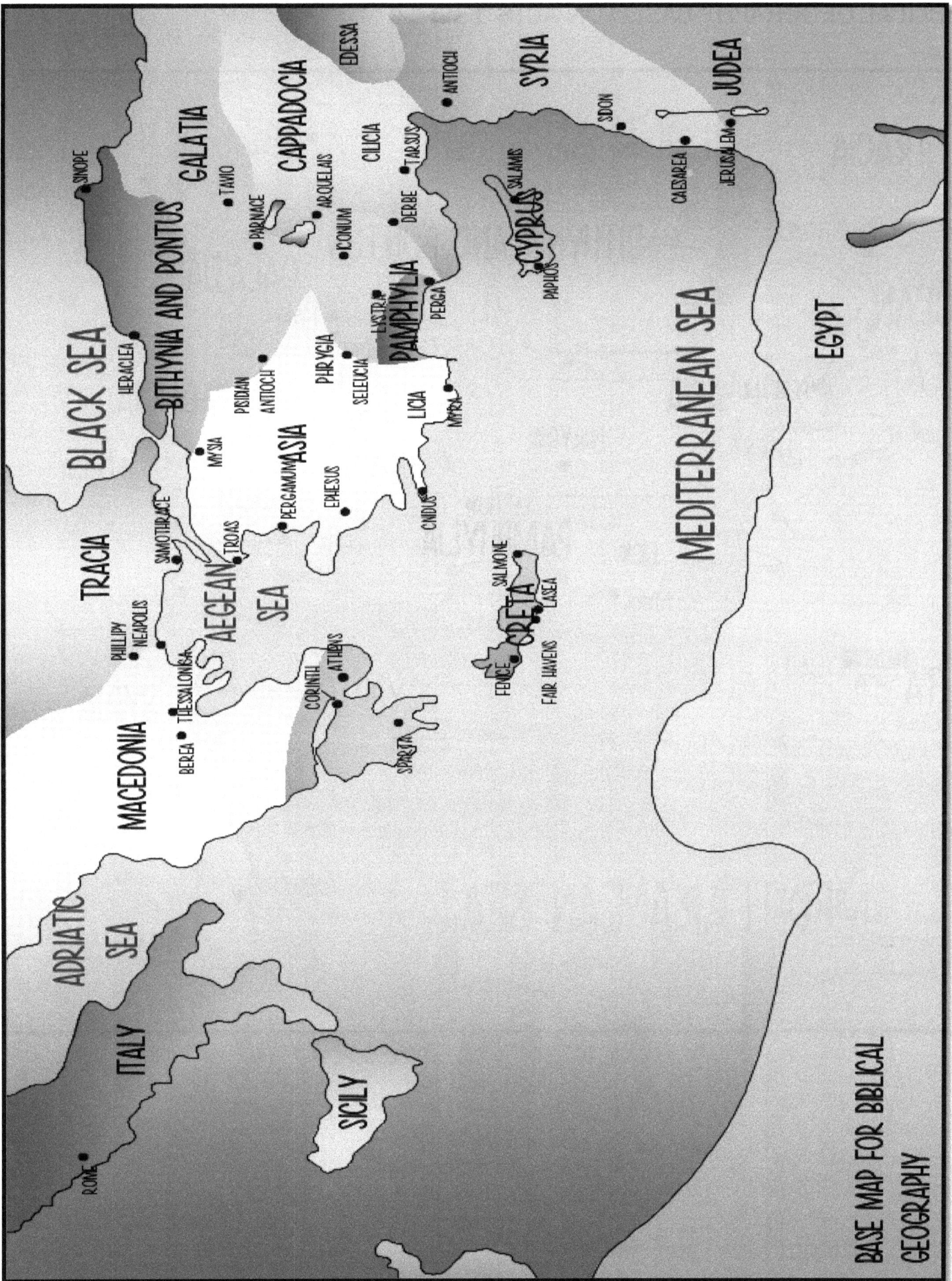

BASE MAP FOR BIBLICAL GEOGRAPHY

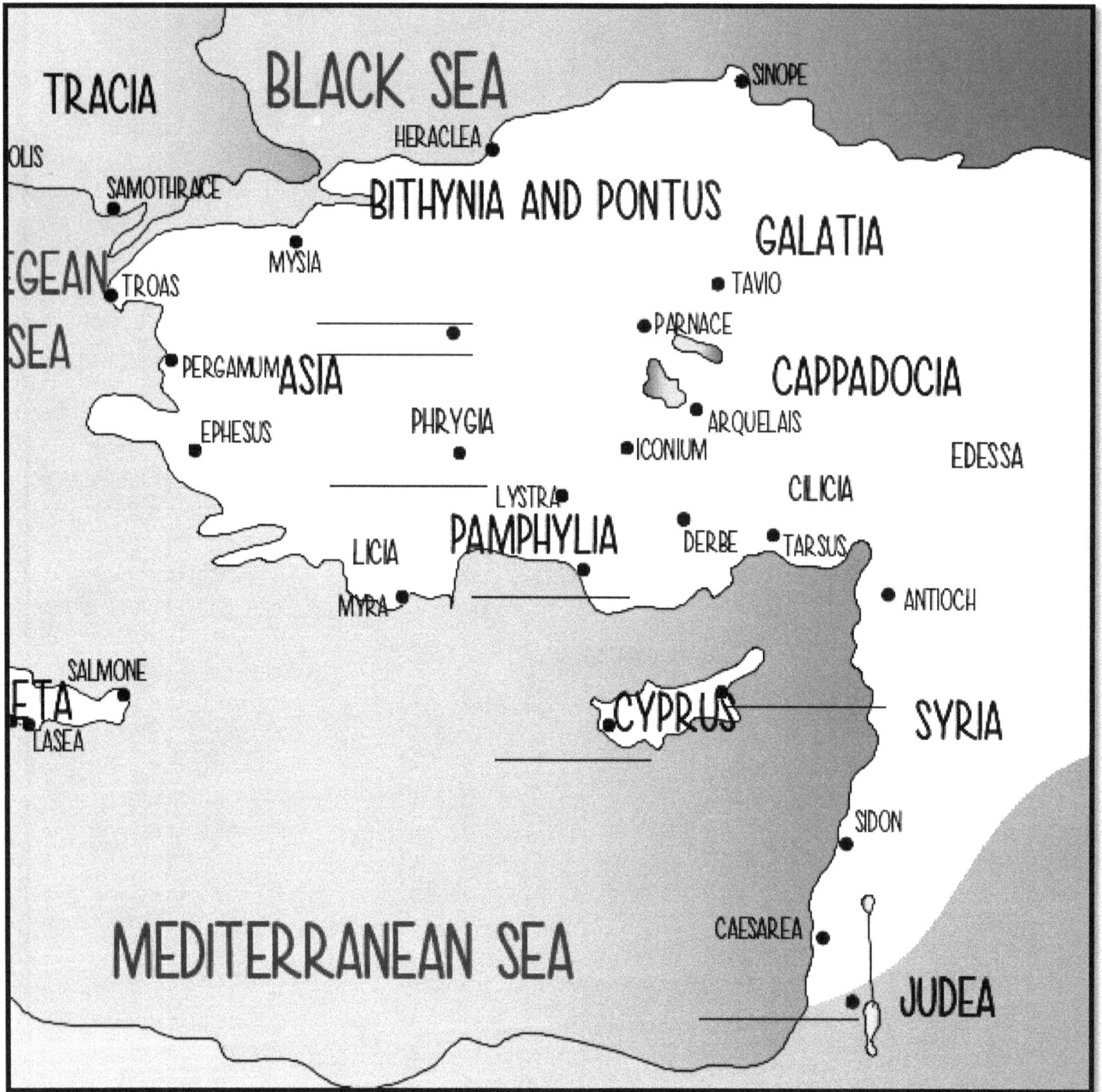

TRACIA

BLACK SEA

SINOPE

HERACLEA

BITHYNIA AND PONTUS

GALATIA

OLIS

SAMOTHRACE

TAVIO

EGEAN

MYSIA

TROAS

PARNACE

SEA

CAPPADOCIA

PERGAMUM ASIA

PHRYGIA

EPHESUS

ARQUELAIS

ICONIUM

EDESSA

LYSTRA

CILICIA

PAMPHYLIA

DERBE

TARSUS

LICIA

ANTIOCH

MYRA

SALMONE

ETA

CYPRUS

SYRIA

LASEA

SIDON

CAESAREA

MEDITERRANEAN SEA

JUDEA

BIBLICAL GEOGRAPHY BASED ON ACTS 16:1-12

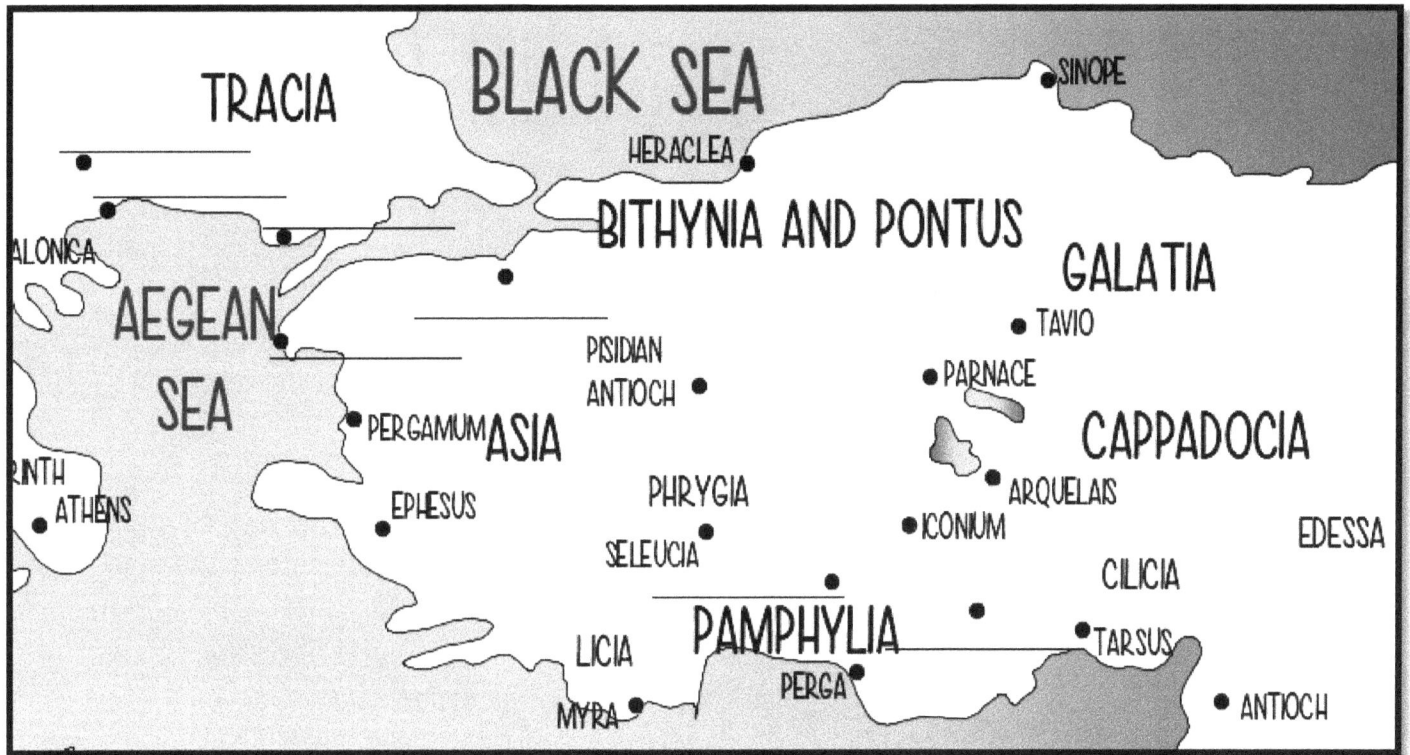

BIBLICAL GEOGRAPHY BASED ON ACTS 27:3-12

MEMORY

INSTRUCTIONS:

1. The teams will have 5 minutes to connect the pairs on the floor or table.

2. If more than one team correctly connects all 8 pairs, the team that does it first will be awarded 10 bonus points. The judge will also give 10 points to each team for each of their correct pairs.

CONSULTATIONS:

The participants cannot consult with their coach or with other members of their team; only among themselves.

FOUL:

If someone from the audience says a verse or reference, the judge will subtract 10 points from the team.

EXAMPLE:

But you will receive power when the Holy Spirit comes on you; and you will be my witnesses in Jerusalem, and in all Judea and Samaria, and to the ends of the earth.	ACTS 1:8
They devoted themselves to the apostles' teaching and to fellowship, to the breaking of bread and to prayer.	ACTS 2:42

MAGIC WORD

INSTRUCTIONS:

1. No team may see the puzzle before the competition is started. The game is played simultaneously by all participating teams. Each team will work on a different puzzle, but with the same number of letters. The search starts from the letter with the star, and the participants must draw a line in any direction, even diagonally, to join the letters and find the word. The letter must be adjacent horizontally, vertically, or diagonally to connect. When a participant finds the word, he must write it on the line below the puzzle and have a judge verify it.

2. Once the word puzzles are placed on the wall, blackboard or table, the game is started immediately. No team may see the puzzle before the competition is started.

3. The first participant to correctly discover and connect the letters for the word within the time limit wins. The judges must record the time that each puzzle is completed in case there is a disagreement of who finished first. If there is a tie, 10 points is awarded to each team. If a participant incorrectly does their puzzle, the judge who checks it indicates that it is incorrect, and the team is immediately disqualified, and the game continues with the rest of the participants.

4. If none of the teams manage to discover the word, no team receives points.

CONSULTATIONS:
Not permitted.

FOUL:
If anyone present says the word aloud, the judge will indicate it. This game is void, and no team gets points. The game is restarted with a new word game for each team.

EXAMPLE:

POINTS
10 points

TIME
1 minute

PARTICIPANTS
1 per team

MODE
Simultaneous - all teams participate at one time

MATERIALS

- A puzzle with the word to decipher for each team (plus a few extras).
- A marker or pen/pencil for each team

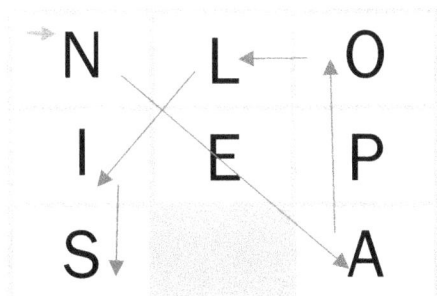

Neapolis

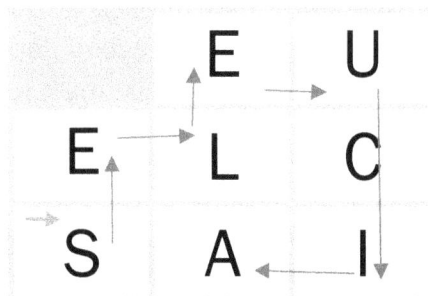

Seleucia

PUZZLES

INSTRUCTIONS:

This competition consists of putting the pieces of the puzzle together on the floor or table. When completed, it should form one of the Bible verses that the children have memorized.

1. Participants are situated one behind the other in their teams, three meters away from the puzzle.

2. Participating teams begin at the same time.

3. The first participant from each team takes a spoon and puts it in his mouth, and then puts the lemon or ball on the spoon in his mouth. The participant then goes to the puzzle, places the spoon and the lemon/ball to one side, and then arranges one piece of the puzzle in horizontal form. He then takes the spoon and the lemon/ball and goes back to the next participant on his team and hands him the lemon/ball by passing it with his spoon onto his teammate's spoon.

4. They repeat the same action and so on until the puzzle is finished. (If the child drops the spoon or lemon, he must return to the starting point and start again.

5. The team that finishes first with the correct answer is the winner and receives 30 points. If there is a tie between teams, the 30 points are awarded to each team.

CONSULTATIONS:

Consultation is allowed only among the 3 participants.

FOUL

If a judge observes one of the children holding the lemon/ball or spoon with their hand, or if they throw the spoon or lemon and continue without returning to their place of departure, the judge will inform the moderator, and the child must return to the place of departure to restart the journey.

If one of the participants places more than one piece of the puzzle, the judge will indicate that to the moderator, and the moderator will remove one of the pieces of the puzzle and return it to the pile of pieces.

POINTS
30 points

TIME
There is no time limit. The game ends when one team finishes their puzzle.

PARTICIPANTS
3 per team

MODE
Simultaneous - all teams participate at one time

MATERIALS
- A memory verse divided into 9 pieces, one for each team (the same memory verse for each team)
- 3 spoons per team
- 3 lemons or balls per team
- NOTE: The verse must be taken from the list of memory verses.

EXAMPLE:

AND ENCOURAGED BY	ENJOYED A TIME OF PEACE	LIVING IN THE FEAR OF THE LORD
THEN THE CHURCH THROUGHOUT	THE HOLY SPIRIT	JUDEA, GALILEE AND SAMARIA
IT INCREASED IN NUMBERS	AND WAS STRENGTHENED	ACTS 9:31

THE KEY LETTER

INSTRUCTIONS:

The moderator will give a sealed envelope that will contain a category (characters, places, objects, animals, miscellaneous) and a base vowel to each participating team. The teams will participate simultaneously by writing a list of words related to the selected category containing the specific base letter they received in their envelope.

1. Each team will choose an envelope containing a category and base letter from the moderator.
2. The 3 participants will form a line three meters away from the board. When the moderator gives the signal, the first participant of each team goes to the board and writes a qualifying word, then returns to their team and hands the marker/chalk to the next participant of his team.
3. That second participant then goes to the board and writes the second word and so on until the time limit of one minute is over.

NOTE:

The participant can run or walk to and from the board.

CONSULTATIONS:

Not permitted.

FOUL:

If the judge observes that the participants of a team are speaking among themselves, the value of a word is deducted. If someone from the audience says a word in a loud voice, a judge will indicate it and the value of a word is deducted from all teams.

EXAMPLE:

TEAM "Paul" has the category "Person" with the base vowel A.
TEAM "Missionaries of Jesus" has the category "Places" with the base vowel E.

POINTS
5 points for each correct word

TIME
1 minute

PARTICIPANTS
3 per team

MODE
Simultaneous - all teams participate at one time

MATERIALS

- Sealed envelopes that contain a category (characters, places, objects, animals, miscellaneous) and a base vowel for each participating team
- Chalk boards, white boards, or large pieces of paper - enough for all teams to write on at the same time.
- A marker for each team

PERSON "A"

```
          A
     P  a  u  l
  S  i  l  a  s
D  o  r  c  a  s
     M  a  t  t  h  i  a  s
```

PLACES "E"

```
          E
E  p  h  e  s  i  a  n  s
A  t  h  e  n  s
S  e  l  e  u  c  i  a
L  a  s  e  a
C  r  e  t  e
```

FINISH THE STORY

INSTRUCTIONS:

The moderator will have a list of biblical passages to read, one for each participating team. The biblical passages must be different, but they must have the same number of verses.

1. The moderator draws the order of participation.

2. The 3 participants of the first team will sit in the three chairs. The moderator begins by reading the biblical passage to the first team. As soon as one of the three participants of the team recognizes what passage it refers to, they must interrupt the moderator by rising from their place to continue the story. The time begins the moment the moderator starts reading and stops when the participant gets up. The judges record this time. The moderator instructs the participant to finish the story. The participant has 1 minute to do so.

3. When the participant finishes the story, the moderator announces if the rest of the story is correct or not, and the time obtained. If the story is not correct, the moderator announces "INCORRECT." If 2 or 3 participants of the team get up at the same time, they must immediately decide which participant will continue.

4. The moderator then repeats the process with a different passage for the next team.

5. The winning team is the one who correctly finishes the story and has the shortest time elapsed during the reading of the moderator. The time judge must make sure that the participant does not exceed the 1-minute time limit to complete the story.

CONSULTATIONS:

Quiet consultation between the 3 participants of the team is allowed.

FOUL:

If one of the participants gets up from his place to finish the story, but forgets the rest of the story, he is given 15 seconds to start his response. If he remains silent or sits down again, the judge indicates "INCORRECT" to the moderator, ending the participation of that team in this game.

SUGGESTION DE PASAJES BÍBLICOS:

- Jesus taken to heaven, Acts 1:1-11
- The Holy Spirit descends during Pentecost, Acts 2:1-12
- Ananias y Sapphira, Acts 5:1-11
- The conversion of Saul, Acts 9:1-19
- Priscilla, Aquila & Apollos, Acts 18:18-28

30 points

1 minute

3 per team

MODE

One team at a time

MATERIALS

- One biblical passage for each team. Each passage must be different, but the same number of verses.
- Three chairs

ALPHABET SOUP

INSTRUCTIONS:

Each team will receive the same puzzle at the same time.

Each team must discover the words that appear horizontally, vertically, diagonally, top to bottom, left to right or vice versa.

1. The moderator places the puzzles face down on the table or floor in front of each team. The puzzles must have in the title a topic related to the search, for example: Paul's companions, Places where Paul went, Objects, etc.

2. When the start signal is given, each team must turn over the puzzle and find the words. Words must be circled and written down on the side of the puzzle.

3. When a team finishes, they must take their completed puzzle to one of the judges for review (the time is recorded). (The other teams continue working on their puzzles.) If the judge observes that the team has found all of the correct words, he/she will inform the moderator. The competition stops and one of the participants reads the list aloud and that team wins 50 points.

4. If the word puzzle is incorrect on some word(s), the judge will simply say "Incorrect" and the team will continue to search for words

The maximum time for this competition is 7 minutes. If no team finishes during the set time, the competition is scored according to the correct answers (5 points per correct answer).

CONSULTATIONS:

Consultation on the puzzle will only be between the two participants of the team.

FOUL:

If a participant consults with someone other than their other participating teammate, the judge will indicate it and give them a 30-second penalty.

POINTS
50 points, or 5 points for each correct word

TIME
7 minutes

PARTICIPANTS
2 per team

MODE
Simultaneous - all teams participate at one time

MATERIALS
- A marker or pencil per team.
- Word-search puzzles with ten words to discover – sufficient number for each participating team to receive one copy.

EXAMPLE:

Alphabet Soup for "Paul's Companions"

S	R	T	L	S	U	C	I	H	C	Y	T
A	R	J	Y	E	R	O	P	T	B	A	M
Q	F	T	D	T	F	S	I	L	A	S	E
U	T	G	I	R	V	M	F	R	R	W	S
I	G	N	A	M	O	S	A	V	N	L	O
L	B	M	N	T	O	T	Y	M	A	T	L
A	N	B	A	R	N	T	B	A	B	O	L
T	H	O	V	B	N	M	H	A	U	G	O
Y	O	Q	W	E	R	T	Y	Y	S	A	P
U	J	H	P	R	I	S	C	I	L	L	A
I	H	C	V	A	R	T	Y	I	O	E	U
S	O	P	A	T	E	R	B	G	A	S	J

AQUILA

LYDIA

APOLLOS

TYCHICUS

SILAS

BARNABUS

PRISCILLA

SOPATER

TIMOTHY

JOHN

REFLECTION CATEGORY

The coach facilitates the lesson considering the objective or purpose of the teaching, and dialogues with the children of the team allowing them to formulate their questions. The objective of this category is to motivate the boys and girls to reflective on the Bible reading in terms of the spiritual teachings it contains, and the context (historical, cultural, idiomatic, etc.) in which it is developed.

Let children know that learning is the result of personal effort.

SOME REFLECTION TECHNIQUES:

- Dialogue

- Directed Questions

- Active listening and intense participation

- Focus on the essentials

- Harmonize theory and practice

For a local, district, zone, national demonstration, etc. the moderator will choose

2 reflection games

The teams will find out which games will be played only on the day of the demonstrations.

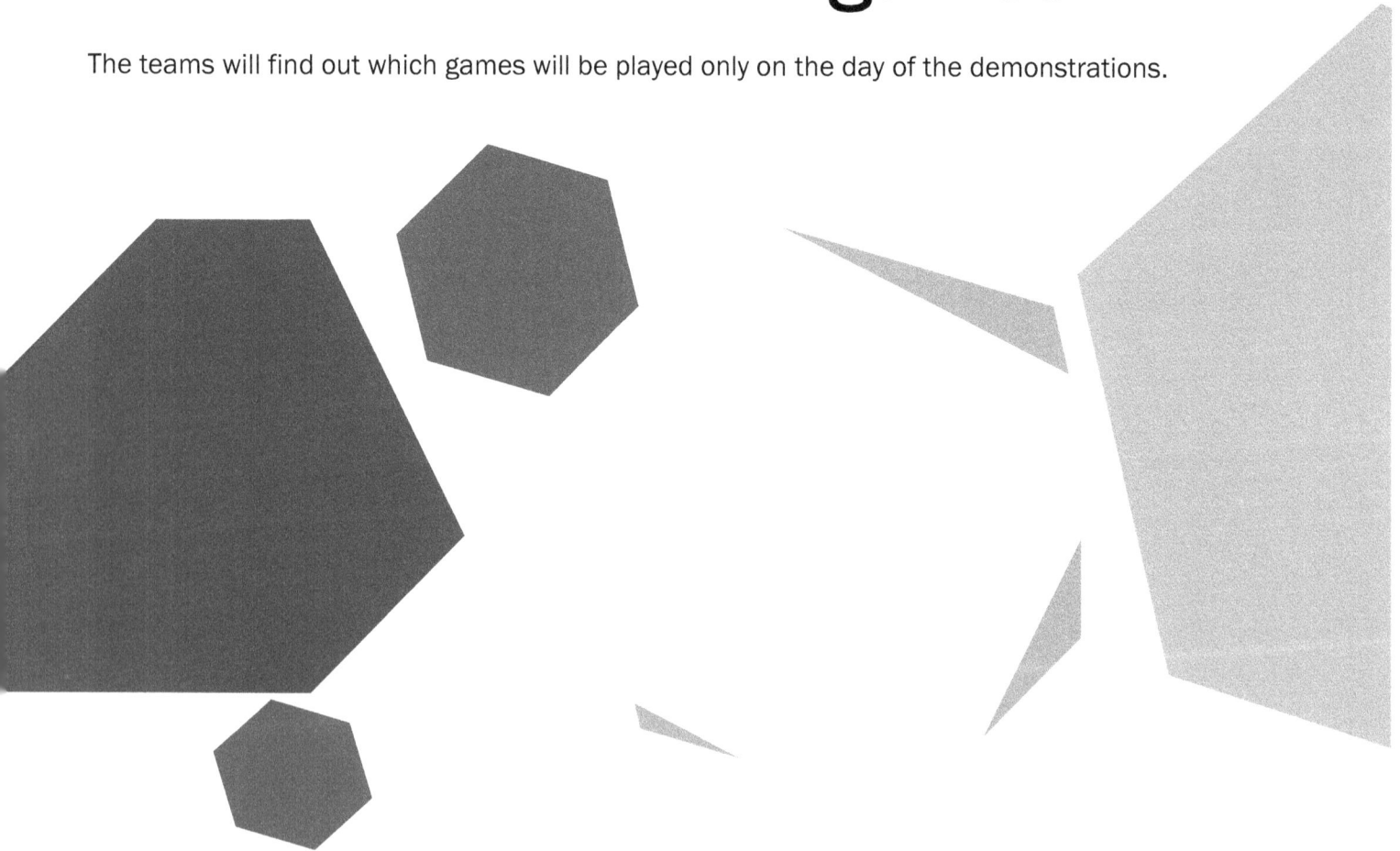

HELP THE MISSIONARIES

INSTRUCTIONS:

1. The moderator determines the order of participation.

2. The participant selects an envelope, each envelope contains a case study and two biblical verses. The moderator places the 2 biblical verses on the board 2-3 meters away from the participant.

3. The moderator will read the case study aloud and then the verses.

4. The participant chooses which verse he considers appropriate for the case study. He then explains the reason for his answer. He has 1 minute to give his answer.

5. If the answer is correct, the judge scores 20 points for the team. If the answer is incorrect, the moderator will say the correct verse in relation to the case.

6. If the participant chooses the correct verse, but the explanation is not correct, his team only gets 10 points.

FOUL:

If someone in the audience or team says the answer out loud or tries to help the participant, the judge tells the moderator and 10 points are deducted from the team score.

EXAMPLE:

My friend Silvia just went as a missionary to Mexico for a short time. She had many ideas that she wanted to work on there, but the pastor of the church didn't allow her to do them. This discouraged her.

Answers:

1. "The following night the Lord stood near Paul and said, 'Take courage! As you have testified about me in Jerusalem, so you must also testify in Rome.'" (Acts 23:11)

2. "You stiff-necked people! Your hearts and ears are still uncircumcised. You are just like your ancestors: You always resist the Holy Spirit!" (Acts 7:51)

POINTS
20 points

TIME
1 minute

PARTICIPANTS
1 per team

MODE
One team at a time

MATERIALS

- 1 Envelope for each team, containing case studies of missionaries, preferable real.

- Two Bible verses for each case; one must be related to the case and another must not be. They should be printed on letter size paper so that the participants can read them from where they will be standing.

CHEST OF MEMORIES

INSTRUCTIONS:

The moderator will place the objects inside the chest/trunk/box beforehand.

1. Each team will choose a participation number.

2. Starting with team 1, the moderator will invite the first participant to put his hand into the chest and take out an object without looking. The participant then will have 2 minutes to explain what that object represents from the Bible verses being studied.

3. If the participant relates his story well, the judge will give him 10 points, and then continue on to the second participant of the same team. The same directions apply to the second participant, as well as to additional teams. Each participant can earn 10 points, for a maximum of 20 points per team.

NOTE:

An object that has been taken out of the chest is not put back in after the participant is finished with it.

CONSULTATIONS:

Not permitted.

FOUL:

If a participant consults with his partner or anyone else, the judge will deduct 10 points from the team.

POINTS
10 points for explaining correctly

TIME
2 minutes

PARTICIPANTS
2 per team

MODE
One team at a time

MATERIALS

- Objects of any material
- A wooden chest or trunk, or one made out of cardboard
- Participation numbers

EXAMPLE:

Birds	10:12, 11:6	Table	06:02
Anchor	27:13, 29, 30, 40	Clouds	1:9 2:19
Boat	20:38, Cap. 27	Bread	12:3, 20:6 3:2, 3:10
Chains	12:6-7, 16:26	Gate	12:13-16
Bed	9:33-34, 12:20, 28:8	Planks	27:44
House	2:2, 2:46, 9:11, 9:43	Cloth	16:14
Belt	21:01	Tent	18:03
Sword	12:2, 16:27	Bulls	14:13
Island	13:6, 21:3	Window	20:09

HOW DO YOU IMAGINE IT? (NEW GAME)

INSTRUCTIONS:

1. The moderator draws the order of participation and allows the participants to choose a random envelope.
2. The moderator opens the envelope of the first participant and reads the place, and the child has a minute to give the name of the event that happened in that place and a description of what he imagines that place was like.
3. The judge evaluates both the name of the event and the description of the place according to the study book. If both are correct, the team receives 30 points.
4. If the participant only says what event happened in the place, 10 points are recorded. If the participant does not respond during the minute, the points are not recorded and the moderator gives the answer.

CONSULTATIONS:
Not permitted.

FOUL:
If the child consults with the coach or with other members of his TEAM or if someone in the audience says something out loud, the judge indicates it and that person's participation in this game is canceled.

POINTS
30 points

TIME
1 minute

PARTICIPANTS
1 per team

MODE
One team at a time

MATERIALS
One envelope per team with a place name where an important event happened.

SUGGESTION OF PLACES:

PLACE	EVENT	DESCRIPTION
Gate called Beautiful, Acts 3:1-10	Peter healed a crippled beggar	Let the children to use their imagination to describe what the place might have been like.
Solomon's Colonnade, Acts 3:11-26	Peter addressed the spectators	
Desert road that goes down from Jerusalem to Gaza, Acts 8:26-40	Philip's meeting with the Ethiopian Eunuch	
The banks of the river in Philippi, Acts 16:11-15	Lydia's conversion	
The Areopagus, Acts 17:16-28	Paul defends the gospel before the Athenians	

BIBLE BINGO

INSTRUCTIONS:

(This is similar to the popular game BINGO, using words instead of numbers, and one must fill up the whole card, not just a row.)

The moderator will prepare ½ or ¼ page sized game cards with 9 squares drawn on them for each participant (see next page for an example). Each square will have 1 word in it. All of the words will be different words taken from the scripture passage to be read by the moderator. 8 out of the 9 words will be different than all of the other words on all of the other game cards that all of the other participants have. However, the 9th word in each group will contain the same word – it will be the last word of the biblical passage. (Look at the example on the next page.) You can see that every word on every game card is different except the key word, which is the last word of the passage, which is "SAFELY."

1. When it is time to start, each participant will place their game card and small game pieces in front of themselves on the table, and familiarize themselves with the words on their game card.

2. The moderator will begin to read the chosen biblical passage. (The passage must be no shorter than ten verses and cannot last for more than 3 minutes.) While the moderator reads, the participants must listen carefully to the reading. When the moderator reads a word that is written on a participant's game card, that participant will place one of their game pieces/markers on their game card. (Similar to the game BINGO.)

3. Whoever fills her/his game card first and yells out "FINISHED" will receive 30 points for their team.

NOTE: If there is a tie between teams, 30 points will be awarded to each team. If there is a tie between 2 participants of the same team, only 30 points are given. If at the end of the passage reading, no participant has completely filled their card, nobody gets points.

CONSULTATIONS:

Not permitted.

FOUL:

If a team interrupts or asks questions during the reading, the judge will take away 2 points from that team.

POINTS
30 points

TIME
The length of the reading

PARTICIPANTS
2 per team

MODE
Simultaneous - all teams participate at one time

MATERIALS
- Selected Bible passage
- 2 Game cards for each team
- 9 small objects for each participant that will be used as game pieces or markers (beans, corn, buttons, bottle caps, plastic disks, etc.)

SUGGESTION OF BIBLICAL PASSAGES

- In Athens, Acts 17:16-34
- On the way to Jerusalem, Acts 21:1-15
- The shipwreck, Acts 27:27-44

EXAMPLES OF GAME CARDS:

These examples of game cards are based on the biblical passage
of the shipwreck (Acts 27:27-44), and the key word is "SAFELY."

BIBLICAL PASSAGE: "The Shipwreck" (Acts 27:27-44)

Night	Soundings	God
Eat	Aground	Sea
Safely	Lifeboat	Dawn

Feet	Ship	Hair
Grain	Rudders	Paul
Safely	Adriatic Sea	Food

Sailors	Sandbar	276
Bay	Rocks	Head
Soldiers	Prisoners	Safely

Anchors	Beach	Wind
Swim	Land	Bow
Safely	Ropes	Bread

MODERN DAY BIBLE

INSTRUCTIONS:

Ahead of time, the moderator prepares sealed envelopes containing the bible references for the biblical passage to be narrated, and a participation number on the outside. This bible reference will be different for each team.

1. Each team will choose an envelope.

2. When the start is called, the first team has 2 minutes to open their envelope and look up the Bible verse and discuss the passage together. After 2 minutes, the participants must close their Bible and can no longer look at it or talk among themselves about it. The 3 participants decide who will be their presenter. The presenter then has 1 minute to tell a modern-day version of the story as if it were happening today.

3. When Team 1 is finishes, the moderator will have team two open their envelope and so on.

4. Each team who successfully tells the story will receive 30 points.

CONSULTATIONS:

They can consult the bible and talk between the three team members for 2 minutes.

FOUL:

If the participants consult among themselves after the 2 minutes is finished, or with anyone else during their turn, their team will be disqualified, and no points will be awarded to the team.

SUGGESTIONS OF BIBLICAL PASSAGES:

- Ananias & Sapphira, Acts 5:1-11
- The conversion of Saul, Acts 9:1-19
- In Antioch of Pisidia, Acts 13:13-25
- Paul in the Areopagus, Acts 17:16-28
- Priscilla, Aquila and Apollos, Acts 18:18-28

POINTS
30 points

TIME
3 minutes (2 for consulting the Bible, 1 to tell the story)

PARTICIPANTS
3 per team

MODE
One team at a time

MATERIALS
• An envelope with a different bible passage for each team, with a participation number written on the outside.

THE SHIPWRECK (NEW GAME)

INSTRUCTIONS:

1. The moderator draws the order of participation.
2. The box or boat, which contains several words, is placed on the ground. All participants will have 30 seconds to search for a word related to the shipwreck that is narrated in Acts 27:27-44. At the end of 30 seconds, the judge will check if the word is according to the Biblical passage. If it is correct, 10 points are recorded for the Team.
3. They go one by one according to the order of participation and the moderator asks two questions related to the word:
   - In what verse does it appear?
   - How would you use it, if you were in a shipwreck?

10 points are scored for each correct answer.

If the participant selects a word that has no relation to the passage or if at the end of time he did not get any word related to the subject, the judge indicates it and the boy or girl lose their participation in the game.

FOUL:

If the child pushes another participant during the search, consults with the coach or other members of their team, or if an audience present says something out loud, the judge indicates it and their participation in this game is forfeited.

EXAMPLE:

Some words that can include the shipwreck are: lifeboat, anchors, boat, ropes, bread, wheat, rudders, planks.

It should also include words that have no relation to the subject such as property, fabrics, women, silver, gold, garlands, etc.

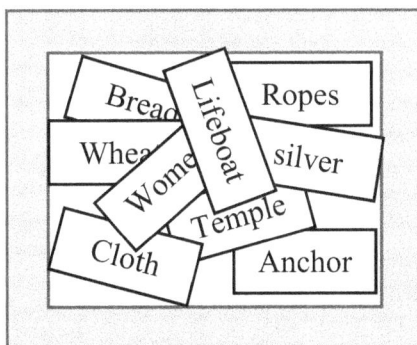

POINTS
10 points if the word is correct, 10 points if the verse location is correct, and 10 points for a good use of the item

TIME
30 seconds to search for the words, and 1 minute for each answer

PARTICIPANTS
1 per team

MODE
Simultaneous - all teams participate at one time searching for the words, and one team at a time responding

MATERIALS
• A plastic or cardboard box (you can also make a boat out of cardboard) • Various slips of paper with words including the objects that appear in the Biblical passage of the shipwreck.

Bread, Lifeboat, Ropes, Wheat, Women, silver, Temple, Cloth, Anchor

Mary from Team "Missionaries for Jesus", got the word "ropes". She replied that it is in verse 32, and she would use it to tie a plank and use it to swim to the beach. The judge considered that it is correct and scored 30 points for her team.	Louis from Team "Paul" got the word, "rudders." He didn't answer in which verse the word was found. He said he would use it to steer the ship and get safely to the beach. The judge gave them 20 points.

Explosions (NEW GAME)

INSTRUCTIONS:

1. The moderator draws the order of participation and participants are placed below their corresponding balloon number.

2. The moderator pops the balloon of the first participant and reads the value that was inside. The participant has two minutes to give a brief explanation of the value, and recite a Bible verse that is associated with the value.

3. The judge evaluates if both the explanation of the value and the biblical text are correct and are associated with the subject of study. If so, the team receives 20 points.

4. If the child correctly explains what the value is, but does not say a memory verse (or vice versa), or the verse has no relation to the value, the team only receives 10 points.

CONSULTATIONS:
Not permitted.

FOUL:
If the child consults with the coach or with other members of his team or if the audience says something out loud, the judge indicates it and that person's participation in this game is canceled.

WHAT ARE VALUES?
Values are principles that guide our lives (conduct).

LIST OF VALUES:
Generosity, respect, gratitude, friendship, responsibility, peace, solidarity, tolerance, honesty, justice, freedom, strength, loyalty, integrity, forgiveness, kindness, humility, perseverance, love, unity, trust.

POINTS
20 points

TIME
2 minutes

PARTICIPANTS
1 per team

MODE
One team at a time

MATERIALS

- A rope or yarn.
- One blown-up balloon per team. Inside the balloon there must be a small piece of paper with the name of a value. To make it more fun you can also place confetti.
- A needle for popping the balloons.

EXAMPLE:

Generosity	"They sold property and possessions to give to anyone who had need." Acts 2:45
Gratitude	"After he said this, he took some bread and gave thanks to God in front of them all. Then he broke it and began to eat." Acts 27:35
Hospitality	"When she and the members of her household were baptized, she invited us to her home. 'If you consider me a believer in the Lord,' she said, 'come and stay at my house.' And she persuaded us." Acts 16:15

FOLLOWING THE FOOTPRINTS

INSTRUCTIONS:

1. All teams will choose an envelope from the moderator and then line up at the START in front of the giant footprints on the floor.
2. The moderator will receive the envelope from team #1 and ask a question from the questions inside to the participant from team #1. The participant has 30 seconds to give the answer. If in 30 seconds they correctly answer the question, they put their color card on the first footprint. If they don't give the correct answer or remain silent, the moderator will say the correct answer and they won't be able to advance.
3. Then the moderator will receive the envelope from the second team and ask that team's participant the first question from that list, and so forth through the teams.
4. Once all teams have been asked question 1, the moderator begins again with team #1 by asking their question #2 and so forth. When a team answers correctly, they advance their colored card marker along the footprints. When a team answers incorrectly, they don't move their colored card marker.
5. The game is over after 12 questions have been asked to each participant. Teams that answer all 12 questions correctly will reach footprint #12 and receive 60 points. All other teams will receive 5 points for each correct answer they give.

CONSULTATIONS:

Not permitted.

FOUL:

If someone from the audience says the answer aloud, 10 points will be deducted from the team that committed this infraction.

EXAMPLE:

POINTS

5 points for each correct answer

TIME

30 seconds to give their answer

PARTICIPANTS

1 per team

MODE

One team at a time, alternating

MATERIALS

- The moderator will prepare a questionnaire with 12 different questions for each team and put it in a sealed numbered envelope.
- 12 FOOTPRINTS made of any material
- 2 signs, one that says "START," the other "FINISH,"
- a different colored card for each team.
-

Isabel from Team "Paul" answered 9 questions earning 45 points for her Team.

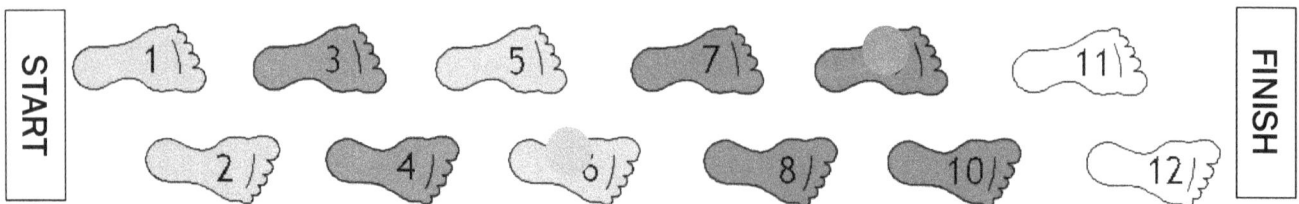

Camila from Team "Acts that transform" answered 6 questions earning 30 points for her Team.

ARTS & CRAFTS CATEGORY

Crafts can also be used as teaching tools, helping the children with their personal creativity development, as well as a form of recreation. Crafts are used in the early stages of learning because they help with the development of gross and fine motor skills.

This category will help the children represent biblical knowledge through different arts and crafts expressions.

IDEAS:

- Ask your local SDMI president to supply you with teaching materials, paper of different colors and textures, scissors, glue, yarn, glitter, straws, finger paint, paints, brushes, etc.

- Do activities that allow children to develop their creativity.

For a local, district, zone, national demonstration, etc. the moderator will choose:

1 Arts and Crafts game

The teams will know the game that will be played only on the day of the demonstration.

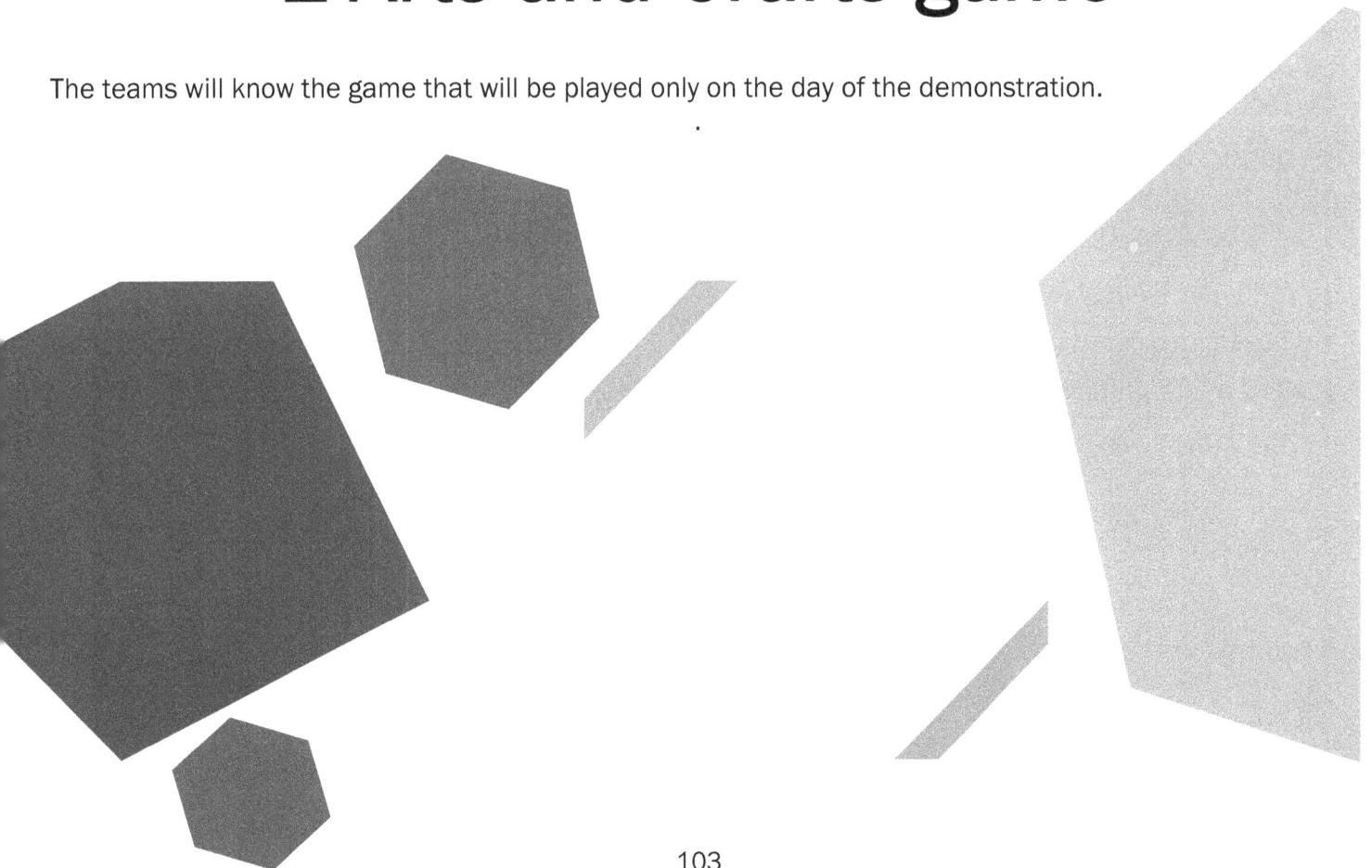

FLAGS

INSTRUCTIONS:

1. Each team will receive an envelope and materials to create their flag. When the moderator gives the signal, each team will have 5 minutes to create a flag that somehow illustrates the place or character that they received in their envelope.

2. At the end of 5 minutes, all teams will stop working. Then one participant from each team will have 1 minute to explain their flag. This will be done according to their participation number.

The judges will award points based on the following criteria:

- Quality of workmanship and creativity: 5-10 points
- Explanation: 5-10 points
- Good use of the materials: 5-10 points

CONSULTATIONS:

Only among the participants of the team.

FOUL:

If during the explanation, a different participant or a member of the audience speaks, 10 points will be deducted from the team that commits this infraction.

SUGGESTION OF PLACES:

- The Gate called Beautiful: Acts 3:1-10
- Solomon's Colonnade: Acts 3:11-26
- Desert road descending from Jerusalem to Gaza: Acts 8:26-40
- The shores of the river in Philippi: Acts 16:11-15
- The Areopagus: Acts 17:16-28

POINTS
30 points maximum

TIME
5 minutes to make the flag and 1 minute to explain it

PARTICIPANTS
2 per team

MODE
Simultaneous - all teams participate at one time making their flags, and one team at a time explaining them

MATERIALS

- The moderator will prepare 1 card per team, on which is written the name of a place or Bible character from the biblical passages being studied. Each card must be different. These cards are placed in sealed envelopes with a participation number on the outside.

- Sheets of paper, colored paper, wooden or plastic sticks of 60 cm. White glue, scissors, markers.

COLLAGE

INSTRUCTIONS:

1. The moderator will have each team choose an envelope with a theme and participation number.

2. Each team will be given materials and a place to make their collage.

3. The moderator will start the game with a whistle – all teams will participate at the same time. Each team will have 5 minutes to make a collage to illustrate the theme that they received in their envelope. Team members may talk with one another, but not with anyone else.

4. After 5 minutes, all teams will stop working on their collages. Each team will appoint a representative from among the three, who will have 1 minute to explain their collage. Teams will present in the order of their participation number.

THE JUDGES WILL AWARD POINTS BASED ON THE FOLLOWING CRITERIA:

Creativity and good use of colors: 5-10 points

Use of materials: 5-10 points

Explanation: 5-10 points

CONSULTATIONS:

Talking only among the 3 participants of the team.

FOUL:

5 points will be deducted from the team that is talking to each other during the explanation of the collages by any of the participating teams.

SUGGESTION OF THEMES:

- Jesus taken to heaven, Acts 1:1-11
- The Holy Spirit descends at Pentecost, Acts 2:1-12
- Ananias and Sapphira, Acts 5:1-11
- The conversion of Saul, Acts 9:1-19
- Priscilla, Aquila and Apollos, Acts 18:18-28

POINTS
30 points

TIME
5 minutes to make the collage
1 minute to explain it.

PARTICIPANTS
3 per team

MODE
Simultaneous - all teams participate at one time to make their collages, and then 1 team at a time will explain their collage.

MATERIALS
- The moderator will prepare 1 theme for each team in sealed envelopes, with the participation number on the outside.
- Cardboard or letter-sized paper, scissors, white glue, paper of different colors and textures, such as tissue paper, newspaper, etc.

ANSWER AND DRAW

INSTRUCTIONS:

1. The moderator will give each team an envelope containing the base drawing, as well as a theme story and 5 different questions for each team about that story. The envelopes will be numbered on the outside.
2. When it is time for the first team to start, the team will hand their envelope to the moderator, who will tape the base picture to a board or wall that the team can easily reach to draw on.
3. The team will form a line in front of the base drawing with the 5 participants. The moderator will announce their theme story, and then ask the first participant a question from the envelope. When the moderator finishes the first question, the time of 1 minute is started per participant. If the participant answers the question correctly, he will start drawing on the base picture, illustrating the theme story that they have been given. He draws until his minute is up. If the participant answers incorrectly, he does not proceed to draw on the picture, his turn is over, and the moderator continues by asking the next team participant a question. If that participant answers the question correctly, he goes and continues the same drawing that the first person started, and so forth. After all 5 participants of the team have had the opportunity to answer a question and draw, the moderator will ask a team representative to explain the picture they drew (1 minute time limit).
4. After the first team finishes, the moderator moves on to the second team, and so forth.

The judges award points based on these criteria:
- Clarity of the drawing: 5-10 points
- Drawing is relevant to the subject of study: 5-10 points
- The picture is drawn realistically: 5-10 points

CONSULTATIONS:

Not permitted, each participant must answer their question without consulting their teammates.

FOUL:

If another participant answers the question asked to one of their teammates or if someone in the audience says the answer out loud, the participation of this team is canceled for this game only.

SUGGESTION OF THEMES:

1. Jesus taken up into heaven: Acts 1:1-11
2. The Holy Spirit descending during Pentecost: Acts 2:1-12
3. Ananias y Sapphira, Acts 5:1-11
4. The banks of the river in Philippi: Acts 16:11-15
5. The shipwreck: Acts 27:27-44

POINTS
30 points maximum

TIME
3 minutes

PARTICIPANTS
5 per team

MODE
One team at a time

MATERIALS

- The moderator will present a base drawing, such as a prison, city, mountains, sea, etc., on a sheet of paper for each team to draw on. The drawing must be different for each team.
- Colored markers for the team drawing.

DRAW IT

Note: This game is similar to the popular game Pictionary.

INSTRUCTIONS:

1. The moderator will give a sealed envelope containing two themes to each team.
2. When the game begins, the moderator will receive the envelope from team #1 and give one of the themes to one of the participants. That participant will have 1 minute to draw the theme while their teammate tries to figure out what he/she is drawing. If the teammate guesses the theme within the 1 minute time limit, their team receives 15 points. Then the roles are reversed. The guesser now becomes the drawer and receives the other theme from the moderator, and the one who drew first becomes the guesser. Again the time limit is 1 minute, and 15 points goes to the team for a correct answer within the time limit.
3. The same procedure is followed with the following teams until all teams have finished.

CONSULTATIONS:
Not permitted.

FOUL:
If the audience or other team members interrupts by giving any response, the team's participation in that round is canceled and no points are awarded.

SUGGESTION DE TEMAS:

Events
- Jesus taken to heaven, Acts 1:1-11
- The Holy Spirit descends at Pentecost, Acts 2:1-12
- Ananias and Sapphira, Acts 5:1-11
- The conversion of Saul, Acts 9:1-19
- Priscilla, Aquila and Apollos, Acts 18:18-28

Characters
- Paul
- Peter
- Dorcas
- Barnabas
- Philip
- Lydia
- Timothy
- Aquila
- Priscilla

POINTS
30 points (15 for each participant)

TIME
1 minute to draw, 1 minute to say the answer

PARTICIPANTS
2 per team

MODE
One team at a time

MATERIALS

- The moderator will prepare a list of themes (Bible events and characters) from the Bible passages being studied. Two themes, on separate pieces of paper) will be placed into sealed envelopes with a participation number on the outside for each team.
- A large sheet of paper or a blackboard/whiteboard
- Markers or chalk

EMOTION-ART (NEW GAME)

INSTRUCTIONS:

This game was designed with the understanding that the coach of each team should be teaching the children about emotions and how to manage them.

1. The moderator chooses numbers for the order of the teams.

2. Each participant is given a paper with two silhouettes of faces (male/female) and a marker.

3. The moderator will say the name of a character(s) and an event in which the character(s) felt some emotion. For example: "Paul in the Shipwreck."

4. Each participant must draw the facial expressions that correspond to the emotion that the character felt, in this case, the drawing would be done on the male silhouette. They will have 1 minute to do this. (In case you talk about several characters such as guards, church, etc., they can use both silhouettes).

5. After the minute of drawing, according to the order that was drawn, each participant will give an explanation to the judges about the emotion and why they think the character felt it.

For this game, the following evaluation scale is taken into account:
Clarity and quality of the drawing: 5-10 points
Explanation: 5-10 points

CONSULTATIONS:
Not permitted.

FOUL:
If a participant tries to see or replicate what another team is doing, the judge indicates it and their participation in this game is canceled.

SUGGESTION DE TEMAS:
- Galilean men looking to heaven: Acts 1:9-10
- The community of believers: Acts 2:41-47
- The church and all who heard about the death of Ananias and Sapphira: Acts 5: 10-11
- The advocates of circumcision when they learned that the Holy Spirit was poured out on the Gentiles: Acts 10:45
- The guards when they learned that Paul and Silas were Roman citizens: Acts 16:38

POINTS
20 points

TIME
1 minute to draw,
1 minute to explain

PARTICIPANTS
1 per team

MODE
Simultaneous - all teams participate at one time drawing, and one at a time explaining

MATERIALS
- Papers with silhouettes of faces (man / woman) (2 silhouettes per team)
- Markers

annoyed	confused	deceived	disgusted
embarrased	joyful	frustrated	angry
happy	innocent	irritated	lonely
nervios	peaceful	proud	sad
afraid	shocked	sick	joking
amazed	suspicious	tired	worried

PUPPETS

INSTRUCTIONS:

1. The moderator will ask the two participants of each team to sit on the floor or at a table, along with their envelope and supplies.

2. When the moderator blows his whistle, each team will create a puppet that represents their Bible character. At the end of 5 minutes, all the teams must stop working. Then in order of participation number, 1 member from each team will have 1 minute to use their puppet to explain who they are.

The judges will award points based on the follow criteria:

Creativity and workmanship of the puppet: 5-10 points

Creativity in the presentation: 5-10 points

Good use of the materials: 5-10 points

CONSULTATIONS:

Consultations permitted only between the 2 members of the team.

FOUL:

5 points are deducted from teams that talk during the explanation of their character or while other teams are presenting.

NOTE: At the end of the activity, an exhibition can be made to appreciate the work the children did and to reward their creativity.

SUGGESTED CHARACTERS:

- Paul
- Peter
- Dorcas
- Silas
- Barnabas
- Philip
- Lydia
- Timothy
- Aquila
- Priscilla

POINTS
30 points

TIME
5 minutes to make the puppet, 1 minute for the presentation

PARTICIPANTS
2 per team

MODE
Simultaneous - all teams participate at one time making the puppets, and one team at a time for the presentations

MATERIALS
- The moderator will prepare an envelope for each team with the name of the Bible character the team needs to portray and a participation number on the outside. This Bible character must be different for each team.
- Paper bag, white glue, paper of different textures and colors wool or yarn, markers, scissors for each team.

ACTING CATEGORY

The game consists in representing a character in an integral way. For this it is necessary that the actor, the child, knows the character and can express it with his body expressions and voice.

In this category, the objective is to develop in the child the ability to express with his body a spiritual message that involves the study of the Word of God.

SOME IDEAS:

- Create an atmosphere of respect and a positive spirit in the children so that they do not mock or laugh when one of their classmates participates in this category.

- Perform activities that allow the children to gain self-confidence and lose shyness.

For a local, district, zone, national demonstration, etc. the moderator will choose:

1 performance game

The teams will know the game that will be done only on the day of the demonstration.

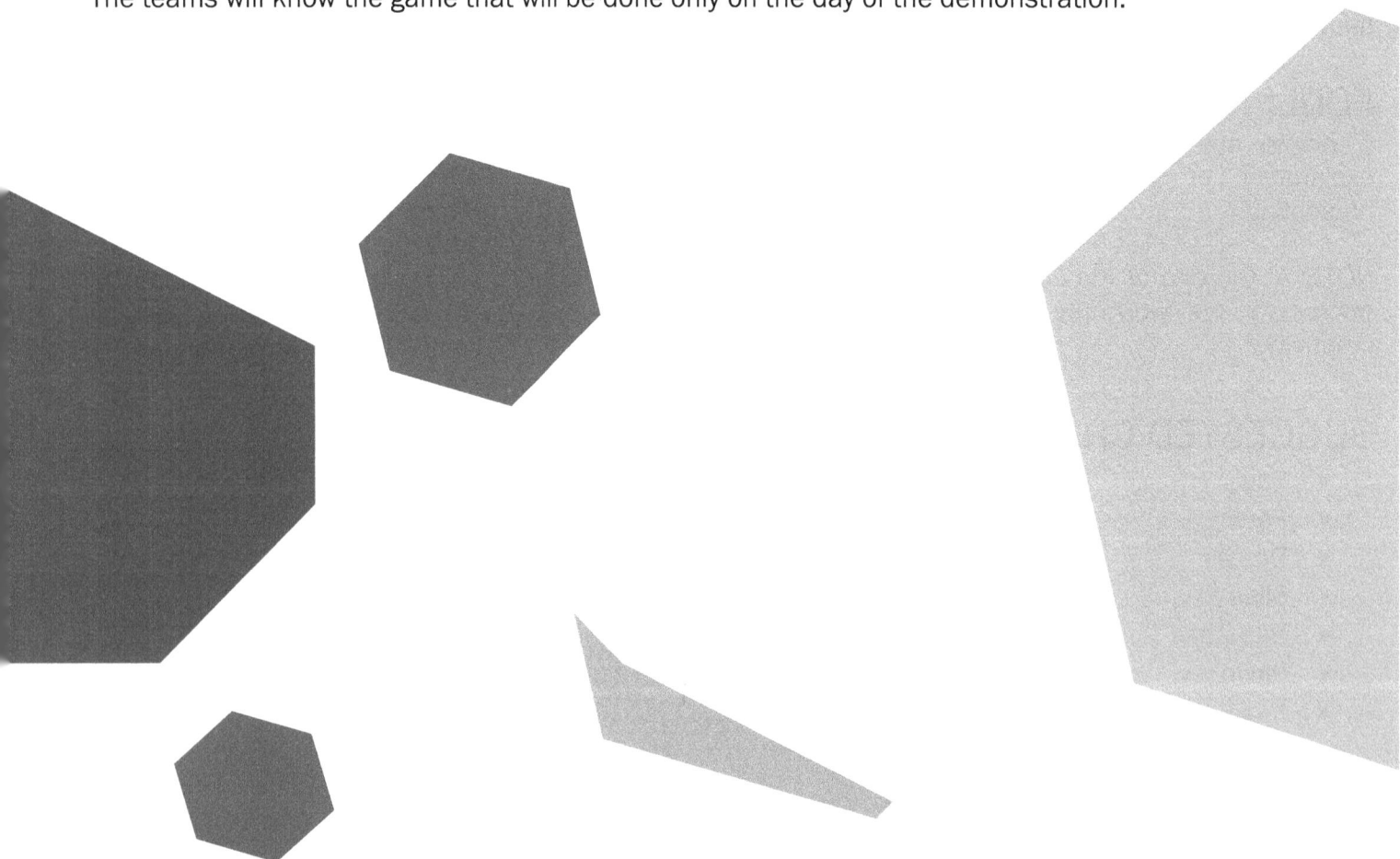

ACROSTIC

INSTRUCTIONS:

1. Each team will receive an envelope with their character name and card.
2. When the moderator gives the start signal, all teams will start at the same time and will have 5 minutes to make an acrostic using the name they received in their envelope (see example below).
3. At the end of the 5 minutes, each team must stop work. Then the moderator will give one participant from each team, 1 minute to present their acrostic (in participation number order).

The judges will award points based on the following criteria:

Gestures: 5-10 points

Coordination between the 2 team members: 5-10 points

Intonation: 5-10 points

Creativity of presentation: 5-10 points

Acrostic related to the theme: 5-10 points

CONSULTATIONS:
Only permitted between the 2 team members.

FOUL:
5 points are deducted from the team that is talking to each other when another team is making its presentation.

SUGGESTED CHARACTERS:
- Paul
- Peter
- Dorcas
- Philip
- Timothy
- Aquila
- Priscilla
- Jesus

J ewels the savior has given me
E ntirely his life he gave
S orry for failing
U nited to you I always want to be
S ilence I will keep when you want to talk to me

POINTS
50 points maximum

TIME
5 minutes to make the acrostic and 1 minute to present it

PARTICIPANTS
2 per team

MODE
Simultaneous - all teams participate at one time making their acrostics, and then one team at a time will make their presentation

MATERIALS
- The moderator will prepare cards (one for each team) on which is written a name of a Bible character that has been studied (a different name for each team). The card, along with a blank card, will be placed in a sealed envelope with a participation number on the outside.

- Markers

POETRY

INSTRUCTIONS:

1. Each team will receive a participation number. The moderator starts with the first team to participate, giving one minute for the 2 participants to present their poem together.

The judges will award points based on the following criteria:

Gestures	5-10 points
Coordination between the 2 members of the team	5-10 points
Intonation	5-10 points
Lyrics	5-10 points
Content related to the study theme	5-10 points

Note: The poem must have 3 stanzas and the presentation must be no longer than 1 minute. It must have been written by the team, and have unpublished lyrics.

CONSULTATIONS:
Not permitted.

FOUL:
5 points will be deducted from a team that is talking to each other when another team is making its presentation.

EXAMPLE:
From his scaled eyes they fell,
it was the transformation Jesus gave him
With new eyes the vision received,
preaching the gospel in every nation
He understood that it was not just for Jews,
for Gentiles as well.
Hallelujah Christ changed him!
Going through the villages,
the streets and the synagogues
with power he gave the Word.
Some listened to him,
others believed
and there were those who persecuted him.
He suffered with patience
what he himself was doing.
Hallelujah Christ changed him!
Towards the end of his days,
he persisted in preaching and teaching,
imprisoned in his home, his disciples sent,
following the example of the teacher,
fulfilling his mission did not tire.
Hallelujah Christ changed him!

POINTS
50 points

TIME
1 minute

PARTICIPANTS
2 per team

MODE
One team at a time

MATERIALS

CHARADES

INSTRUCTIONS:

1. The moderator will write down a theme/Bible story on note cards, a different one per team, and put them in sealed envelopes with participation numbers on the outside. The envelopes must not be opened until it is time for the team to participate.

2. The participant who chooses the envelope must act out the theme/Bible story so that his 4 remaining teammates can try to guess the theme/Bible story he is trying to communicate through his actions. The team has 2 minutes to give the correct answer.

3. The judge awards 25 points if the team answers correctly. If the team answers incorrectly, the judge indicates it and no score is given to that team. The moderator should say the correct answer out loud if it is not guessed.

CONSULTATIONS:

Only among the 4 participants that must guess the theme.

FOUL:

If the audience present or other members of a team interrupt by saying possible answers, the judge indicates it and the moderator cancels the team's participation in this game only.

SUGGESTION OF THEMES:

1. Jesus taken to heaven: Acts 1:1-11

2. The Holy Spirit descends at Pentecost: Acts 2:1-12

3. Ananias and Sapphira: Acts 5:1-11

4. On the banks of the river in Philippi: Acts 16:11-15

5. The Shipwreck: Acts 27:27-44

POINTS
25 points

TIME
2 minutes

PARTICIPANTS
5 per team

MODE
One team at a time

MATERIALS
• 1 envelope for each team with their theme (different for each team) and participation number

DRAMA

INSTRUCTIONS:

1. Each team will choose an envelope.

2. With all teams starting at the same time, the moderator will give the go ahead, and the teams will have 5 minutes to prepare their dramas with the themes that they received in their envelopes. The drama should be presented as if it were happening today in modern times.

3. After the 5 minutes of preparation time, coaches must leave and the teams must present their dramas in the order of their participation numbers. Once team #1 has finished, team #2 will begin, etc....

Note: It's important to take into account that teams must bring their costumes, decorations and other props they wish to use with them to the demonstration.

The judges will award points based on the following criteria:

Participation of the whole team: 5-10 points

The ability to represent the story accurately: 5-10 points

The fluidity of the dialogue: 5-10 points

The use of available resources (props, decorations, etc.): 5-10 pts

The drama is faithful to the teaching of the event/theme: 5-10 pts

CONSULTATIONS:
During the first 5 minutes, they can consult with the coach and among themselves. During the presentation, coaches cannot be consulted.

FOUL:
10 points will be deducted from a team if they speak during another team's presentation

SUGGESTION DE TEMAS:
- Ananias and Sapphira, Acts 5: 1-11
- The conversion of Saul, Acts 9: 1-19
- In Antioch of Pisidia, Acts 13: 13-25
- Paul in the Areopagus, Acts 17: 16-28
- Priscilla, Aquila and Apollos, Acts 18: 18-28
- The Shipwreck, Acts 27: 27-44

POINTS
50 points maximum

TIME
5 minutes to prepare

PARTICIPANTS
The whole team

MODE
Simultaneous - all teams participate at one time preparing their dramas, and one team at a time presenting

MATERIALS
- The moderator will write down a biblical event on cards, a different one for each team, and then place them in sealed envelopes with participation numbers on the outside.

BREAKING NEWS

INSTRUCTIONS:
1. Each team will choose an envelope.

2. When the moderator gives the go ahead, the teams will have 3 minutes to prepare their news report about the event they received in their envelope. After the 3 minutes of preparation time, one of the team participants will have 1 minute to present the news report as informatively, creatively and interestingly as possible.

3. Once team #1 has finished, team #2 will begin.

The judges will award points based on the following criteria:

Creativity	5-10 points
Content related to the study theme	5-10 points
Fluidity of the dialogue	5-10 points

CONSULTATIONS:
Only permitted among the 4 participants during the first 4 minutes. In addition, they can consult their Bibles.

FOUL:
Ten points are deducted from a team that is talking to each other while another team is presenting.

SUGGESTION OF THEMES:
- Ananias and Sapphira, Acts 5: 1-11
- The conversion of Saul, Acts 9: 1-19
- Paul in the Areopagus, Acts 17: 16-28
- Visit of Paul to Troas Acts 20: 7-12
- Conspiracy to kill Paul, Acts 23: 12-22
- Paul before Agrippa, Acts 25: 23-27
- The Shipwreck, Acts 27: 27-44

POINTS
30 points maximum

TIME
4 minutes

PARTICIPANTS
4 per team

MODE
All teams will prepare their newscast at the same time, and then one team at a time will present

MATERIALS
- The moderator will put a biblical event or bible passage on note cards, a different one for each team, and then place them in sealed envelopes with participation numbers on the outside.

- Letter size piece of paper and pencil or pen for each team.

MUSIC CATEGORY

Music is the art of organizing sounds in a sensible and coherent way, with harmony, melody and rhythm. The objective of this category is to teach the child to praise God intelligently, doing so with the knowledge of God's Word, with a biblical foundation and spiritual knowledge.

IDEAS:

- Ask for help from members of the worship ministry.
- Provide small times of praise in your meetings with the team.
- Identify the children with skills on instruments or a good singing voice.
- Allow children to participate in the creation of an unpublished song, thus develop their creativity.

For a local, district, zone, national demonstration, etc. the moderator will choose

1 music game

The teams will know the games that will be played only on the day of the demonstration.

As for the unpublished song, this must be presented in the final demonstration.

SINGING THE VERSE

INSTRUCTIONS:

1. Each team will chose an envelope with their Bible verse and participation number.
2. When the moderator gives the start signal for the first team to start, the team will have 3 minutes to read the verse and then come up with a tune and choreography. The team will then present the "song."

The judges will award points based on the following criteria:

Intonation and harmony: 5-10 points

Creativity in the presentation: 5-10 points

CONSULTATIONS:

They can consult with their coach during the first 3 minutes.

FOUL:

If a team talks while another team is presenting, 10 points will be deducted from the team that commits this infraction.

SUGGESTION OF TEXTS:

Choose a text from the Memory Verse list found on page 57.

POINTS

20 points maximum

TIME

3 minutes

PARTICIPANTS

The whole team

MODE

One team at a time

MATERIALS

- The moderator will prepare a card for each team with Bible verses from the memory verse list (a different one for each team) and put them in sealed envelopes with participation numbers on the outside.

NEW SONG

INSTRUCTIONS:

Each team must present an unpublished song, which will be sung by the whole team. The team can present it with choreography or spiritual dancing, etc. The song must have:

- Unpublished lyrics (lyrics must be written by the team)
- Lyrics related to the theme of Bible Quizzing.
- The actual tune may be from a published Christian song, but the lyrics must be changed.
- Minumum of two verses, maximum of four.
- Maximum duration of three minutes.

1. The moderator will draw the order of participation.
2. Each team will have a maximum of 3 minutes to present their song, ideally with music, and actions.

The judges will award points based on the following criteria:

Quality of the Unpublished lyrics: 5-10 points

Lyrics related to the theme of the Quizzing Study: 5-10 pts

Music (intonation, harmony): 5-10 points

Creativity in the presentation: 5-10 points

Full team participation: 5-10 points

CONSULTATIONS:
Not permitted.

FOUL:
20 points will be deducted from a team that is talking to each other while another team is presenting.

POINTS
50 points maximum

TIME
3 minutes

PARTICIPANTS
The whole team

MODE
One team at a time

MATERIALS

MUSICAL ROULETTE (NEW GAME)

INSTRUCTIONS:

1. The moderator draws the order of participation and places the roulette in front of the spectators.

2. The participants make a line in the order of participation three meters away from the roulette wheel.

3. Each child will rotate the wheel and according to the character that the wheel stops at, he will have a maximum of 1 minute to sing a small musical jingle. (These musical jingles should be prepared in advance with the help of the coach.)

The judges will award points based on the following criteria:

Music (intonation, harmony): 5-10 points

Creativity in the presentation: 5-10 points

CONSULTATIONS:
Not permitted

FOUL:
Ten points are deducted from a team if it is talking to each other while another team is presenting.

SUGGESTIONS OF CHARACTERS:
- Paul
- Peter
- Tabitha
- Philip
- Timothy
- Aquila
- Priscilla

POINTS
20 points maximum

TIME
1 minute

PARTICIPANTS
1 per team

MODE
One team at a time

MATERIALS
• Roulette of Characters

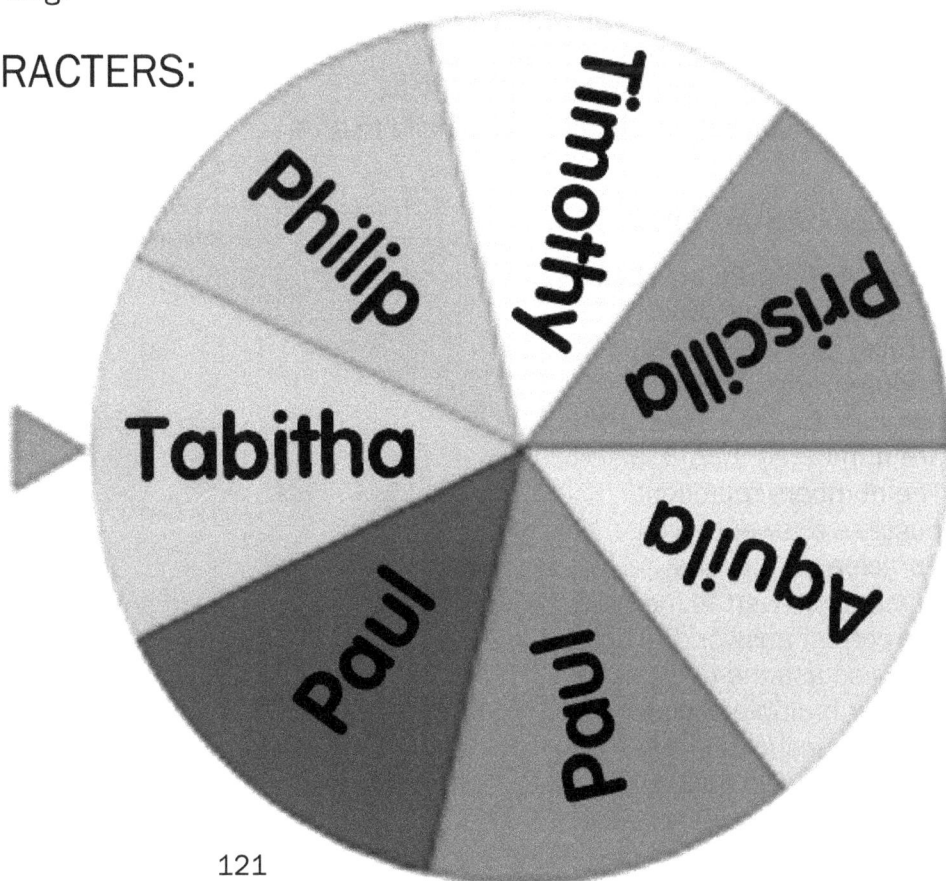

GUIDE FOR CHILDREN'S BIBLE QUIZZING USING QUESTIONS AND ANSWERS

Children's Bible Quizzing is an optional part of Bible Studies for Children. Each church and each child decides whether to participate in a series of competitive events.

Quizzing events follow the rules outlined in this book. Children do not compete against each other to determine a single winner. Churches do not compete against each other to determine a winner.

The purpose of Quizzing is to help the children to determine what they learned about the Bible, to enjoy the competitive events, and to grow in the ability to display Christian attitudes and Christian behaviors during competitive events.

In Quizzing, each child challenges himself or herself to attain an award level. In this approach, children quiz against a base of knowledge, not against each other. Quizzing uses a multiple-choice approach that allows every child to answer every question. Multiple choice questions offer several answers, and the child chooses the correct one. This approach makes it possible for every child to be a winner.

QUIZZING SUPPLIES

Each child uses a quiz box (see picture) (or similar device) to answer questions during events. The quiz box contains four tab inserts that are numbered 1, 2, 3, and 4. The numbers represent possible answer choices. Participants pull one numbered insert to indicate the correct answer. Children can also use the quiz box to answer multiple-choice review questions in the classroom. The quiz box dimensions are 30 cm wide

X 13 cm deep X 28 cm high. Quiz boxes may be purchased from The Foundry (*www.gokidsquiz.com*), or a local team may make their own. For instructions to make quiz boxes, visit *kidzfirstpublications.net*

Each group of children will need a person to score their answers. There is a reproducible score sheet at the end of the book. Use this score sheet to keep track of the answers of each child.

If possible, provide some type of an award for the performance of the children in each Quizzing event. Suggested awards are certificates, stickers, ribbons, trophies, or medals.

Certificate templates are included on pages 58-59.

Please follow these rules. Competitions that do not operate in accordance with the Children's Quizzing Official Competition Rules and Procedures will not qualify for other competition levels.

AGES AND GRADES

Children in grades 1-6 may participate in Children's Quizzing competitions. Seventh graders, regardless of age, participate in Teen Quizzing. (For countries other than the United States, grades 1-6 are generally ages 6-12).

BASIC LEVEL COMPETITION

This competition level is for younger or beginning quizzers. Older quizzers who prefer an easier level of competition may also participate in the Basic Level. The questions for the Basic Level are simpler. There are three answers for each question, and there are fifteen questions in each round. The district or regional Children's

Quizzing director determines the questions and the number of rounds at each Quizzing competition. Most competitions have two or three rounds.

ADVANCED LEVEL COMPETITION

This competition level is for older quizzers or experienced quizzers. Younger quizzers who want a greater challenge may participate in the Advanced Level. The questions for the Advanced Level are more comprehensive. There are four answers for each question, and there are twenty questions in each round. The district or regional Children's Quizzing director determines the questions and the number of rounds at each Quizzing event.

SWITCHING BETWEEN LEVELS

Children may switch between Basic Level and Advanced Level only for invitational Quizzing competitions. This helps the leaders and the children determine the best level for each child.

For the zone/area, the district, and the regional competitions, the local director must register each child for either Basic Level or Advanced Level. The child must compete at the same level for zone/area, district, and regional competitions.

TYPES OF COMPETITION

Invitational Competition

An invitational competition is between two or more churches. Local Children's Quizzing directors, zone/area Children's Quizzing directors, or district Children's Quizzing directors may organize invitational competitions. Individuals who organize an invitational competition have the responsibility to prepare the competition questions.

Zone/Area Competition

Each district may have smaller groupings of churches that are called zones. If one zone has more quizzers than another zone, the district Children's Quizzing director may separate or combine the zones to create areas with a more equitable distribution of quizzers. The term area means combined or divided zones.

The churches located in each zone/area compete in that zone/area. The district Children's Quizzing director organizes the competition. Questions for the zone/area competitions are official questions.

E-mail ChildQuiz@nazarene.org to request these questions from the General Children's Quizzing Office.

District Competition

Children advance from the zone/area competition to the district competition. The district Children's Quizzing director determines the qualifications for the competition and organizes the competition.

Questions for district competitions are official questions. E-mail ChildQuiz@nazarene.org to request these questions from the General Children's Quizzing Office.

Regional Competition

The regional competition is a competition between two or more districts.

When there is a regional Children's Quizzing director, he or she determines the qualifications for the competition and organizes the competition. If there is not a regional director, the participating district directors organize the competition.

Questions for the regional competitions are official questions. To request these questions from the General Children's Quizzing Office, e-mail ChildQuiz@nazarene.org.

WORLD QUIZ COMPETITION

Every four years, the General Children's Quizzing Office in conjunction with Sunday School and Discipleship Ministries International sponsors an international World Quiz. The Global Children's Quizzing Office determines the dates, the locations, the costs, the qualifying dates, and the overall qualifying process for all World Quiz competitions.

E-mail ChildQuiz@nazarene.org for more information.

DISTRICT CHILDREN'S QUIZZING DIRECTOR

The district Children's Quizzing director operates all competitions according to the Children's Quizzing Official Competition Rules and Procedures.

He or she has the authority to introduce additional Quizzing procedures on the district as long as the procedures do not conflict with the Children's Quizzing Official Competition Rules and Procedures. The district Children's Quizzing director contacts the General Children's Quizzing Office, when necessary, to request a specific change in the

Children's Quizzing Official Competition Rules and Procedures for a district. The district Children's Quizzing director makes the decisions and solves the problems within the guidelines of the Children's Quizzing Official Competition Rules and Procedures. The district Children's Quizzing director contacts the General Children's Quizzing Office for an official ruling on a specific situation, if necessary.

REGIONAL CHILDREN'S QUIZZING DIRECTOR

The regional Children's Quizzing director creates a regional Children's Quizzing leadership team that consists of all of the district Children's Quizzing directors on the region. The regional Children's Quizzing director remains in contact with this team to keep the procedures consistent across the region. He or she operates and organizes the regional competitions according to the Children's Quizzing Official Competition Rules and Procedures. The regional Children's Quizzing director contacts the General Children's Quizzing Office to request any changes in the Children's Quizzing Official Competition Rules and Procedures for a specific region. He or she resolves any conflicts that arise with the help of the guidelines of the Children's Quizzing Official Competition Rules and Procedures. The regional Children's Quizzing director contacts the General Children's Quizzing Office for an official ruling on a specific situation, if necessary. He or she contacts the General Children's Quizzing Office to place the regional quiz date on the general church calendar.

In the United States and Canada, the regional Children's Quizzing director is a developing position. Currently that person does not preside over district Children's Quizzing directors on the region.

QUIZMASTER

The quizmaster reads the competition questions at a Quizzing competition. The quizmaster reads the question and the multiple-choice answers two times before the children answer the question. He or she follows the Children's Quizzing Official Competition Rules and Procedures established by the General Children's Quizzing Office and the district Children's Quizzing director/regional coordinator. In the event of a conflict, the final authority is the district/regional Children's Quizzing director who consults the Children's Quizzing Official Competition Rules and Procedures. The quizmaster may participate in discussions with scorekeepers and the district/regional Children's Quizzing director about a challenge. The quizmaster may call a time-out.

SCOREKEEPER

The scorekeeper scores a group of children's answers. He or she may participate in discussions with scorekeepers and the district/regional Children's Quizzing director about a challenge. All scorekeepers are to use the same method and the same symbols to insure correct tabulation of the scores.

SYNOPSIS OF HOW THE QUESTIONS ARE READ AND ANSWERED

The quizmaster reads the question and all answer choices twice. After the quizmaster reads the second time, he or she will call the children to respond. The quizmaster never reads questions once.

- The quizmaster says, "QUESTION" and then reads the question and all answer choices.

- The quizmaster repeats this sequence.

- The quizmaster says, "ANSWER," which prompts the participants' to respond.

Example: The quizmaster says, **"QUESTION: What did Mary name her baby? Answer number one, Joseph. Answer number two, John. Answer number three, Jesus."** The quizmaster briefly pauses and starts again and says, **"QUESTION: What did Mary name her baby? Answer number one, Joseph. Answer number two, John. Answer number three, Jesus."** The quizmaster briefly pauses and calls for the answer and says, **"ANSWER."** The children then indicate their answer choice by removing the number from their box that corresponds to their answer.

The quizmaster *may* read a question a third time for especially difficult or long questions or if a mistake was made when the question was initially read. However, this practice should be the exception, and the participants should be notified of a third repeat in advance to avoid premature responses after the second question and answer sequence.

After the answers are indicated, the quizmaster pauses and watches for the scorekeepers to record all the scores. When the scores are recorded, the quizmaster instructs the children to return their answer numbers to their boxes.

For bonus questions, the quizmaster instructs the team representatives who will answer the bonus question for each team to stand and all the other children to place their hands in their laps. The quizmaster reads the question two times. The child who is ready to answer the bonus question steps to the scorekeepers and quietly gives their answer. The child speaks carefully and quietly so that they do not reveal their answer to other teams. When everyone completes their answer, the quizmaster asks the scorekeepers to raise their hand to reveal who correctly answered. The quizmaster affirms the correct answer or invites a participant to share the correct answer.

When possible, use PowerPoint or other visual media to project questions onto a screen that is visible to all quizzers.

The projected presentation will only include the questions. All answers will be read.

OFFICIAL COMPETITION QUESTIONS

The district Children's Quizzing director is the only individual on the district who may obtain a copy of the official zone/area and district competition questions.

The regional Children's Quizzing director is the only individual on the region who may obtain a copy of the official regional competition questions. If there is not a regional Children's Quizzing director, one participating district Children's Quizzing director may obtain a copy of the official regional competition questions.

Order forms for annual official questions will be sent by E-mail each year. Contact the General Children's Quizzing Office at ChildQuiz@nazarene.org to update your E-mail address. The official questions will arrive by Email to the people who request them.

COMPETITION METHODS

There are two methods of competition.

Individual method

In the individual method of competition, the children compete as individual children. The score of each child is separate from all other scores. Children from the same church may sit together, but do not add together the individual scores to obtain a church or a team score. There are no bonus questions for individual quizzers.

The individual method is the only method to use for the Basic Level competition.

Combination Method

The combination method combines individual and team Quizzing. In this method, churches may send individual quizzers, the teams, or a combination of these to a competition.

The district Children's Quizzing director determines the number of children needed to form a team. All teams must have the same number of quizzers. The recommended number for a team is four or five children.

The children from the churches that do not have enough quizzers to form a team can compete as individual quizzers.

In the combination method, teams qualify for bonus questions. The bonus points awarded for a correct answer to a bonus question become part of the total score of the team, instead of a score for an individual quizzer. There are bonus questions with the official questions for zone/area, district, and regional competitions. Bonus questions typically involve the recitation of a memory verse.

The district Children's Quizzing director selects either the individual method or the combination method for the Advanced Level of the competition.

TIE SCORES

Ties between individual quizzers or the teams remain as tied scores. All individual children or teams who tie receive the same recognition, the same award, and the same advancement to the next level of competition.

BONUS QUESTIONS

Bonus questions are part of the Advanced Level, but only with teams, not individuals. Teams must qualify for a bonus question. Bonus questions occur after questions 5, 10, 15, and 20.

To qualify for a bonus question, a team may have only as many incorrect answers as there are members on the team. For example, a team of four members may have four or fewer answers that are incorrect. A team of five members may have five or fewer answers that are incorrect.

The bonus points for a correct answer become part of the total score of the team, not of the individual score of a child.

The district Children's Quizzing director determines the way that the children answer bonus questions. In most situations, the child verbally gives the answer to the scorekeeper.

Prior to the reading of the bonus question, the local Children's Quizzing director selects one team member to answer the bonus question. The same child may answer all of the bonus questions in a game, or a different child may answer each bonus question.

TIME-OUTS

The district Children's Quizzing director determines the number of time-outs for each church. Each church receives the same number of time-outs, regardless of the number of individual quizzers or teams from that church. For example, if the district director decides to give one time-out, each church receives one timeout.

The district Children's Quizzing director determines if an automatic time-out will occur during the game and the specific point at which the time-out will occur in each game.

The local Children's Quizzing director is the only individual who may call a time-out for a local church team.

The district Children's Quizzing director or quizmaster may call a time-out at any time.

The district Children's Quizzing director, prior to the start of the competition, determines the maximum length of the time-outs for the competition.

SCORING

There are two methods for scoring. The district Children's Quizzing director selects the method.

Five Points

• Award five points for every correct answer. For example, if a child answers 20 questions correctly in an Advanced Level round, the child earns a total of 100 points.

• Award five points for every correct bonus answer in an Advanced Level team Quizzing round. For example, if every member of a team with four persons answers 20 questions correctly in an Advanced Level round and the team answers four bonus questions correctly, the team earns a total of 420 points. Basic Level points will be lower as there are only 15 questions per round, and it is individual competition only.

One Point

Award one point for each correct answer as follows:

• Award one point for every correct answer. For example, if a child answers 20 questions correctly in an Advanced level round, the child earns a total of 20 points.

• Award one point for every correct bonus answer in an Advanced Level team Quizzing round. For example, if every member of a team with four persons answers 20 questions correctly in an Advanced Level round and the team answers four bonus questions correctly, the team earns a total of 84 points.

Basic Level points will be lower as there are only 15 questions per round, and it is individual competition only.

CHALLENGES

Challenges are to be an exception and are not common during a competition.

Request a challenge only when the answer marked as correct in the questions is actually incorrect according to the Bible reference given for that question. Challenges issued for any other reason are invalid.

A quizzer, a Children's Quizzing director, or any other competition participant may not request a challenge because they dislike the wording of a question or answer or think a question is too difficult or confusing.

The local Children's Quizzing director is the only person who may issue a challenge to a competition question. If an individual other than the local Children's Quizzing director attempts to issue a challenge, the challenge is automatically ruled as "invalid."

Individuals who issue invalid challenges disrupt competition and cause the children to lose their concentration. Individuals who consistently issue invalid challenges or create some problems by arguing about a challenge ruling will lose their privilege of challenging the questions for the remainder of the competition.

The district Children's Quizzing director, or the quizmaster in the absence of the district Children's Quizzing director, has the authority to remove the privilege of challenging questions from any or all individuals who abuse the privilege.

The district Children's Quizzing director determines how to challenge a competition question prior to the start of the competition.

• Will the challenge be written or verbal?

• When can a person challenge (during a game or at the end of a game)?

The district Children's Quizzing director should explain the procedure for the challenges to local Children's Quizzing directors at the beginning of the quiz year.

The quizmaster and district Children's Quizzing director follow these steps to rule the challenge.

• Determine if the challenge is valid or invalid. To do this, listen to the reason for the challenge. If the reason is valid, the answer given as the correct answer is incorrect according to the Bible reference, follow the challenge procedures outlined by the district.

• If the reason for the challenge is invalid, announce that the challenge is invalid, and the competition continues.

If more than one person challenges the same question, the quizmaster or district Children's Quizzing director selects one local quiz director to explain the reason for a challenge. After a question has one challenge, another person may not challenge the same question.

If a challenge is valid, the district Children's Quizzing director, or quizmaster in the director's absence, determines how to handle the challenged question. Select one of the following options.

Option A: Eliminate the question, and do not replace it. The result is that a game of 20 questions becomes a game of 19 questions.

Option B: Give every child the points he or she would receive for a correct answer to the challenged question.

Option C: Replace the challenged question. Ask the quizzers a new question.

Option D: Let the children who gave the answer that was listed as the correct answer in the official questions keep their points. Give another question to the children who gave an answer that was an incorrect answer.

AWARD LEVELS

Children's Quizzing has the philosophy that every child has an opportunity to answer every question, and every child receives recognition for every correct answer he or she gives. Therefore, Children's Quizzing uses multiple-choice competition, and ties are never broken.

Children and churches do not compete against each other. They compete to reach an award level. All of the children and all of the churches who reach the same award level receive the same award. Ties remain as tied scores.

Recommended Award Levels:

> Bronze Award = 70-79% correct
>
> Silver Award = 80-89% correct
>
> Gold Award = 90-99% correct
>
> Gold All Star = 100% correct

Resolve all scoring and challenge decisions before presenting awards. The quizmaster and scorekeepers should be sure that all final scores are accurate prior to the presentation.

Never take an award from a child after the child receives an award. If there is a mistake, children may receive a higher award but not a lower award. This is true for individual awards and team awards.

COMPETITION ETHICS

The district Children's Quizzing director is the person on the district who has the responsibility to conduct the competitions in accordance with the Children's Quizzing Official Competition Rules and Procedures.

• *Hearing Questions Before the Competition.* Since competitions use the same questions, it is not appropriate for the children and the workers to attend another zone/area, district, or regional competition prior to their participation in their own competition of the same level. If an adult Quizzing worker attends another competition, the district Children's Quizzing director may choose to disqualify the church from participation in their competition. If a parent and/or child attends another competition, the district Children's Quizzing director may choose to disqualify the church from participation in their competition.

• *Worker's Conduct and Attitudes.* Adults are to conduct themselves in a professional and in a Christian manner. The discussions about disagreements with the district Children's Quizzing director, quizmaster, or scorekeepers are to be private. Adult Quizzing workers should not share information about the disagreement with the children. A cooperative spirit and good

sportsmanship are important. The decisions and the rulings of the district Children's Quizzing director are final. Relay these decisions in a positive tone to the children and to the adults.

CHEATING

Any cheating is serious. Treat the cheating seriously.

The district Children's Quizzing director, in discussion with the district Children's Ministries Council, determines the policy to follow in the event that a child or an adult cheats during a competition.

Make sure that all local children's ministries directors, children's pastors, and local Children's Quizzing directors receive the policy and the procedures of the district. Before accusing an adult or a child of cheating, have some evidence or a witness that the cheating occurred.

Ensure that the quiz continues and that the person accused of cheating does not suffer

embarrassment in front of other people. Here is a sample procedure.

• If you suspect that a child cheated, ask someone to serve as a judge to watch the areas, but do not point out any child whom you suspect. After a few questions, ask the opinion of the judge. If the judge did not see any cheating, continue with the quiz.

• If the judge saw a child who was cheating, ask the judge to affirm it. Do not act until everyone is sure.

• Explain the problem to the local Children's Quizzing director, and ask the director to talk with the accused person privately.

• The quizmaster, the judge, and the local Children's Quizzing director should watch for continued cheating.

• If the cheating continues, the quizmaster and the local Children's Quizzing director should talk with the accused person privately.

• If the cheating continues, the quizmaster should tell the local Children's Quizzing director that he or she will eliminate the score of the child from official competition.

• In the case that a scorekeeper cheated, the district Children's Quizzing director will ask the scorekeeper to leave, and a new scorekeeper will take his or her place.

• In the case that someone in the audience cheated, the district Children's Quizzing director will handle the situation in the most appropriate manner.

UNRESOLVED DECISIONS

Consult with the General Children's Quizzing Office regarding unresolved decisions.

Additional Resources

Additional resources can be downloaded at: *www.SdmiResources.MesoamericaRegion.org*

QUESTIONS FOR BASIC AND ADVANCED COMPETITIONS
(Answers are in *italics*)

Acts 1:1 - 2:47
Basic Competition
To prepare the children for competition, read Acts 1:1-11; 2:1-8, 12-21, 36-47 to them.

1. To whom is the book of Acts written? (1:1)
1. Caesar
2. Luke
3. *Theophilus*

2. About what did Jesus speak when he appeared to the apostles for forty days? (1:3)
1. *About the kingdom of God*
2. About his resurrection
3. About his miracles

3. While he ate with the apostles, Jesus told them not to do something. What was it? (1:4)
1. Do not eat too much.
2. *Do not leave Jerusalem.*
3. Do not tell anyone that you saw me.

4. With what did John baptize? (1:5)
1. With the Holy Spirit
2. With oil
3. *With water*

5. Jesus said that the apostles would receive something after the Holy Spirit came on them. What was it? (1:8)
1. Love
2. *Power*
3. Gifts

6. Jesus said that the apostles would be his witnesses when the Holy Spirit came. Where were they to be witnesses? (1:8)
1. In Jerusalem, in Judea, and in Samaria
2. To the ends of the earth
3. *Both answers are correct.*

7. Who will prophesy when God pours out his Spirit on all people? (2:17-18)
1. Sons and daughters
2. God's servants, both men and women
3. *Both answers are correct.*

8. How many were added to the number of the Apostles on the day of Pentecost? (2:41)
1. About 1,000
2. *About 3,000*
3. About 5,000

9. To what did the believers devote themselves? (2:42)
1. To fellowship and prayer
2. To the breaking of bread
3. *Both answers are correct.*

10. How often did the believers meet? (2:46)
1. *Every day*
2. Only on Sundays
3. Once each week

Advanced Competition
1. While he ate with the apostles, what did Jesus say to them? (1:4-5)
1. "Do not leave Jerusalem."
2. "Wait for the gift my Father promised."
3. "You will be baptized with the Holy Spirit."
4. *All of the answers are correct.*

2. Jesus said that the apostles would be his witnesses when the Holy Spirit came. Where were they to be witnesses? (1:8)
1. In Jerusalem
2. In all Judea and Samaria
3. To the ends of the earth
4. *All of the answers are correct.*

3. What did the two men dressed in white say? (1:11)
1. "Do not be afraid."
2. *"Jesus will come back in the same way you have seen him go into heaven."*
3. "Go to your homes. There is nothing to see here."
4. "Jesus went away to prepare a place for you."

4. What happened when the day of Pentecost came? (2:1-4)
1. They heard a sound like the blowing of a violent wind.
2. They saw tongues of fire that separated and came to rest on each of them.
3. They were filled with the Holy Spirit and began to speak in other tongues.
4. *All of the answers are correct.*

5. Who were staying in Jerusalem on the day of Pentecost? (2:5)
1. Cornelius and his family
2. *God-fearing Jews from every nation*
3. Jesus and the apostles
4. Three women named Mary

6. Peter quotes from an Old Testament prophet on the day of Pentecost. Which prophet was it? (2:16-21)
1. Isaiah
2. Jeremiah
3. *Joel*
4. Samuel

7. Of what did Peter say that Israel should be assured? (2:36)
1. *"God has made this Jesus, whom you crucified, both Lord and Christ."*
2. "John is the only one who should baptize people."
3. "Jesus will tell us about his return."
4. "We apostles saw Jesus."

8. For whom is the promised Holy Spirit? (2:38-39)
1. For you and your children
2. For all who are far off
3. For all whom the Lord our God will call
4. *All of the answers are correct.*

9. What did the believers do after they sold their possessions and goods? (2:45)
1. *They gave to anyone who had a need.*
2. They kept the money for themselves.
3. They gave their money to the church.
4. They bought other things.

10. Finish this verse: "We are witnesses of these things, and so is the Holy Spirit, whom God has given ..." (Acts 5:32)
1. *"... to those who obey him."*
2. "... to those who call on his name."
3. "... to everyone who asks."
4. "... to those who received his spirit."

Acts 3-4:22
Basic Competition
To prepare the children for competition, read Acts 3:1-16; 4:1-22 to them.

1. When did Peter and John go to the Temple? (3:1)
1. At the time of prayer
2. At three o'clock in the afternoon
3. *Both answers are correct.*

2. What was the name of the temple gate? (3:2)
1. Gorgeous
2. *Beautiful*
3. Handsome

3. What happened after Peter took the crippled man by the hand? (3:7-8)
1. *The crippled man jumped to his feet and began to walk.*
2. The crippled man fell down and cried.
3. Peter carried the crippled man into the temple courts.

4. By faith in the name of Jesus, what happened to the crippled man? (3:16)
1. He became a preacher.
2. *The man was made strong.*
3. He received a lot of money.

5. What did the priests, the captain of the temple guard, and the Sadducees do with Peter and John? (4:1-3)
1. They tried to kill them.
2. They paid them for healing the crippled man.
3. *They seized them and put them in jail.*

6. The number of believers grew after Peter and John healed the man. To how many people did the number grow? (4:4)
1. *About 5,000*
2. About 7,000
3. About 10,000

7. How does the book of Acts describe Peter when he spoke to the rulers and elders of the people? (4:8)
1. Peter was excited.
2. *Peter was filled with the Holy Spirit*
3. Peter was afraid.

8. Who is the stone that the builders rejected, who has become the capstone? (4:10-11)
1. Peter
2. *Jesus*
3. John

9. What happened when the rulers and elders of the people saw the courage of Peter and John? (4:13)
1. They were afraid.
2. They were excited.
3. *They were astonished.*

10. After Peter and John healed the crippled man, what command did the rulers and elders of the people give them? (4:18)
1. "Go home and get some rest."
2. "Share with everyone what you saw and heard."
3. *"Do not speak or teach at all in the name of Jesus."*

Advanced Competition

1. What did the crippled man do at the temple gate called Beautiful? (3:2)
1. He ate there.
2. He sold fruits and vegetables there.
3. *He begged there every day.*
4. He rested there while others worshiped.

2. How much silver and gold did Peter give the crippled man? (3:6)
1. *None*
2. 10 shekels
3. A half-shekel
4. 100 shekels

3. After the crippled man began to walk, what did he do? (3:8)
1. He went with Peter and John into the temple courts.
2. He walked and jumped.
3. He praised God.
4. *All of the answers are correct.*

4. Of what were Peter and John witnesses? (3:15)
1. That the crippled man faked his infirmity
2. That the crippled man was a thief
3. *That God raised Jesus from the dead*
4. That Jesus came back in the same way He was taken up.

5. What made the man strong? (3:16)
1. Magic
2. Medicine
3. *Faith*
4. Peter's own power

6. Peter and John were put in jail. What happened afterwards? (4:3-4)
1. *Many who heard the message believed, and the number of men grew to about five thousand.*
2. The crippled man who was healed went free.
3. Peter and John escaped.
4. All of the answers are correct.

7. In whose name did Peter say that the man was healed? (4:9-10)
1. In Peter's name
2. In God's name
3. In the name of the citizens of Jerusalem
4. *In the name of Jesus Christ of Nazareth*

8. Peter and John said they could not stop speaking about something. What was it? (4:19-20)
1. About the man who was healed
2. About how Jesus ascended into heaven
3. *About what they saw and heard*
4. About the way they were mistreated in jail

9. Why did the rulers allow Peter and John to go free? (4:21)
1. Because Peter and John paid a fine
2. *Because all the people were praising God for what had happened*
3. Because the jail was full
4. Because someone bribed them

10. Finish this verse: "Salvation is found in no one else, for there is no other name under heaven given to men..."(Acts 4:12)
1. "...to which we must obey."
2. "...as strong as the name of Jesus."
3. "...that we must fear."
4. *"...by which we must be saved."*

131

Acts 4:23-5:11

Basic Competition

To prepare the children for competition, read Acts 4:23-5:11 to them.

1. After Peter and John gave their report, the people prayed. What happened afterwards? (4:31)
1. The place where they were meeting was shaken.
2. They were all filled with the Holy Spirit and spoke the word of God boldly.
3. *Both answers are correct.*

2. Who were one in heart and mind? (4:32)
1. The Jews
2. *All the believers*
3. The Gentiles

3. What did the believers do with their possessions? (4:32)
1. *They shared everything they had.*
2. They became selfish and kept everything to themselves.
3. None of them had possessions.

4. How many needy persons were among the believers? (4:34)
1. Just a few
2. Hundreds
3. *None*

5. What does the name Barnabas mean? (4:36)
1. Son of God
2. *Son of Encouragement*
3. Son of Thunder

6. Who sold a piece of property and kept back part of the money? (5:1- 2)
1. *Ananias and Sapphira*
2. Barnabas and Joseph.
3. Both answers are correct.

7. Peter said that Ananias lied. To whom did he lie? (5:3-4)
1. To Peter
2. To his wife, Sapphira
3. *To the Holy Spirit*

8. Peter asked Sapphira, "Is this the price you and Ananias got for the land?" What was Sapphira's answer? (5:7-8)
1. *"Yes, that is the price."*
2. "What did Ananias say?"
3. "No, we received more."

9. What happened to Sapphira? (5:10)
1. She fell at Peter's feet and died.
2. She was buried next to her husband.
3. *Both answers are correct.*

10. Finish this verse: "And do not forget to do good and to share with others, for with such sacrifices..." (Hebrews 13:16)
1. "...you will be rewarded."
2. *"...God is pleased."*
3. "...come great things."

Advanced Competition

1. What did the people do when Peter and John reported all that the chief priests and elders had said to them? (4:23-24)
1. *They raised their voices in prayer to God.*
2. They cried out in disbelief.
3. They tore their clothes and mourned.
4. They celebrated.

2. After Peter and John were released, the people prayed. What happened afterwards? (4:31)
1. The place where they were meeting was shaken.
2. They were all filled with the Holy Spirit.
3. They spoke the word of God boldly.
4. *All of the answers are correct.*

3. Who shared everything they had? (4:32)
1. Only Peter and John
2. Only the women and children
3. *All the believers*
4. No one

4. Who was called Barnabas? (4:36)
1. Peter, one of the apostles
2. *Joseph, a Levite from Cyprus*
3. The high priest
4. The apostle who replaced Judas Iscariot

5. What did Barnabas do with the money from a field that he sold? (4:36-37)
1. He kept all the money for himself.
2. He kept some of the money for himself.
3. He bought a house for the apostles.
4. *He put it at the apostles' feet.*

6. According to Peter, to whom did Ananias lie? (5:3)
1. The apostles
2. His wife, Sapphira
3. *The Holy Spirit*
4. All of the answers are correct

7. When did Ananias fall down and die? (5:3-5)
1. When he saw Peter
2. When Sapphira told him that Peter knew what they had done
3. *After Peter said that Ananias had lied to God*
4. When the apostles asked Peter about the money

8. How much did Sapphira say they got for the land? (5:7-8)
1. Not enough
2. *The amount that Ananias gave to the apostles*
3. More than Ananias gave to the apostles
4. She did not know how much they got for the land.

9. What seized the whole church and all who heard about Ananias and Sapphira? (5:11)
1. An overwhelming peace
2. *A great fear*
3. A fierce anger
4. A sense of pride

10. According to Hebrews 13:16, what should we not forget?
1. To say our prayers before bed each night
2. To give all our money to the poor
3. *To do good and to share with others*
4. To read the Bible and to go to church

Acts 6-8:3
Basic competition
To prepare the children for competition, read
Acts 6:1-15; 7:51—8:3 to them.

1. What were the Grecian Jews complaining about? (6:1)
1. Their men did not have enough work.
2. *Their widows were overlooked.*
3. Both answers are correct.

2. Who was a man full of faith and of the Holy Spirit? (6:5)
1. *Stephen*
2. Nicolas
3. Philip

3. Against what could the members of the Synagogue of the Freedmen not stand up? (6:9-10)
1. The wisdom of Stephen
2. The Spirit by whom Stephen spoke
3. *Both answers are correct.*

4. When the Sanhedrin looked intently at Stephen, they noticed something about his face. What was it? (6:15)
1. His face was full of fear.
2. *His face was like the face of an angel.*
3. His face showed no emotion.

5. How were the members of the Sanhedrin just like their fathers? (7:51)
1. *They always resisted the Holy Spirit.*
2. They did not give food to the widows.
3. They always followed the Holy Spirit.

6. What did Stephen see when he looked up to heaven? (7:55-56)
1. He saw the angels bowing at the feet of God.
2. *He saw the Son of Man standing at the right hand of God.*
3. He saw the apostles next to Jesus.

7. What did Stephen pray while he was being stoned? (7:59)
1. "Lord Jesus, take this punishment from me."
2. "Lord Jesus, punish these people."
3. *"Lord Jesus, receive my spirit."*

8. Who gave approval to Stephen's death? (8:1)
1. *Saul*
2. Peter
3. John

9. What happened on the day of Stephen's death? (8:1)
1. Many people became sick and died.
2. The Holy Spirit filled all the believers.
3. *A great persecution broke out against the church in Jerusalem.*

10. After Stephen's death, what did Saul do? (8:3)
1. He began to destroy the church.
2. Going from house to house, he dragged off men and women and put them in prison.
3. *Both answers are correct.*

Advanced Competition

1. How does the book of Acts describe Stephen? (6:5)
1. *A man full of faith and of the Holy Spirit*
2. A wealthy man with a lot of property
3. A man with an unimportant job
4. All of the answers are correct.

2. What happened when the members from the Synagogue of the Freedmen tried to argue with Stephen? (6:9-10)
1. They won their arguments.
2. *They could not stand up against his wisdom or the Spirit by whom he spoke.*
3. Stephen became angry and argued with them.
4. The Lord struck them down.

3. What were some men persuaded to say about Stephen? (6:11)
1. *"We have heard Stephen speak words of blasphemy against Moses and against God."*
2. "Stephen did nothing wrong; let him continue working among us."
3. "Take Stephen and his lies away from us."
4. "Every word that Stephen speaks is true."

4. What did those who were sitting in the Sanhedrin see when they looked intently at Stephen? (6:15)
1. They saw that his eyes were closed.
2. They saw him laughing.
3. They saw angels surrounding him.
4. *They saw that his face was like the face of an angel.*

5. What did Stephen do when he was full of the Holy Spirit? (7:55)
1. He looked up to heaven.
2. He saw the glory of God.
3. He saw Jesus standing at the right hand of God.
4. *All of the answers are correct.*

6. What did the witnesses of Stephen's stoning do? (7:58)
1. They prayed for Stephen.
2. They cried out in anguish.
3. They cheered for those who were stoning him.
4. *They laid their clothes at the feet of Saul.*

7. What did Stephen cry out when he fell on his knees? (7:60)
1. "Lord, punish them for this sin against me."
2. "Lord, please help me."
3. *"Lord, do not hold this sin against them."*
4. "Lord, protect the other believers."

8. Who were scattered throughout Judea and Samaria because a great persecution broke out against the church in Jerusalem?
1. *Everyone except the apostles.*
2. Only Phillip and Stephen.
3. All the Jews.
4. No one.

9. What did Saul begin to do after Stephen's death? (8:3)
1. Destroy the church
2. Go from house to house
3. Drag off men and women and put them in prison.
4. *All of the answers are correct.*

10. Finish this verse: "Blessed is the man who perseveres under trial, because when he has stood the test, he will receive..." (James 1:12)
1. "... immeasurable rewards and eternal life."
2. *"... the crown of life that God has promised to those who love him."*
3. "... all that he desires."
4. "... ten times what he sacrificed."

Acts 8:4-40

Basic Competition
To prepare the children for competition, read Acts 8:4-40 to them.

1. What did Philip do in Samaria? (8:5)
1. He worked for the city.
2. *He proclaimed about Christ.*
3. He practiced sorcery.

2. Who practiced sorcery in the city of Samaria? (8:9)
1. *Simon*
2. Philip
3. Saul

3. Why did people follow Simon the sorcerer? (8:9-11)
1. Because he could heal them
2. *Because he amazed them for a long time with his magic*
3. Because he gave them a lot of money

4. What happened when Peter and John placed their hands on the new believers of Samaria? (8:17)
1. *They received the Holy Spirit*
2. They heard the sound of a violent wind
3. Nothing

5. What did Simon do when he saw that the Spirit was given at the laying on of hands? (8:18)
1. He offered to become a disciple of Peter and John.
2. *He offered Peter and John money.*
3. He laid his hands on Peter and John.

6. What did Peter tell Simon the sorcerer to do after he tried to pay to receive the Holy Spirit? (8:20-22)
1. "Repent of the wickedness."
2. "Pray to the Lord."
3. *Both answers are correct.*

7. What was the Ethiopian doing when Philip met him? (8:28)
1. Sleeping
2. *Reading the book of Isaiah*
3. Begging for money

8. Who told Philip to go to the Ethiopian's chariot and stay near it? (8:29)
1. An angel of the Lord
2. *The Spirit*
3. Peter

9. Who baptized the Ethiopian? (8:38)
1. John
2. Simon
3. *Philip*

10. What did the Ethiopian do after he was baptized? (8:39)
1. *He went on his way rejoicing.*
2. He went away sad.
3. Both answers are correct.

Advanced competition

1. What did those who had been scattered do wherever they went? (8:4)
1. *They preached the word.*
2. They hid in their homes.
3. They prayed that God would destroy their enemies
4. All of the answers are correct.

2. Why did the people follow Simon? (8:11)
1. *He amazed them for a long time with his magic.*
2. He paid them to follow him.
3. He preached about Christ.
4. All of the answers are correct.

3. What did the men and women do when they believed Philip and his preaching? (8:12)
1. They stoned Simon.
2. They gave all their money to the poor.
3. They dedicated their children to God.
4. *They were baptized.*

4. What did Simon want the apostles to give him? (8:18-19)
1. *The ability so that everyone he laid his hands on would receive the Holy Spirit*
2. The ability to preach like the apostles
3. The secrets of the apostles
4. The Holy Spirit

5. What did Peter say to Simon when he tried to buy the gift of God with money? (8:20-23)
1. "You have no part or share in this ministry."
2. "Your heart is not right before God."
3. "Repent of this wickedness and pray to the Lord."
4. *All of the answers are correct.*

6. Why did the Ethiopian eunuch go to Jerusalem? (8:27)
1. To sign agreements between his country and Jerusalem
2. To visit Candace, queen of the Ethiopians
3. To purchase food and clothing
4. *To worship*

7. What was the Ethiopian reading when Philip met him? (8:28)
1. The book of Revelation
2. *The book of Isaiah*
3. Treasury reports
4. The book of Jeremiah

8. What did Philip tell the Ethiopian when he asked about the person mentioned in the book of Isaiah? (8:34-35)
1. *Philip told him the good news of Jesus.*
2. Philip told him about Stephen's stoning.
3. Philip told him that he did not understand what the prophet meant.
4. Philip told him that he must first be baptized.

9. Where did Philip appear after he baptized the Ethiopian? (8:40)
1. *In Azotus*
2. In Samaria
3. In Ethiopia
4. In Jerusalem

10. According to Psalm 119:130, what gives light and understanding to the simple? (Psalm 119:130)
1. The sun
2. A picture of Jesus
3. *The unfolding of God's words*
4. The moon and stars

Acts 9:1-31
Basic competition
To prepare the children for competition, read Acts 9:1-31 to them.

1. Who breathed out murderous threats against the Lord's disciples? (9:1)
1. Philip
2. *Saul*
3. Peter

2. Who said, "Saul, Saul, why do you persecute me?" (9:4-5)
1. Stephen
2. Peter and John
3. *Jesus*

3. What happened when Saul got up from the ground? (9:8)
1. He ran away.
2. *He could not see anything.*
3. He looked for the voice that spoke to him.

4. In Damascus, to whom did the Lord call in a vision? (9:10)
1. The Ethiopian
2. John
3. *Ananias*

5. What did the Lord tell Ananias to do in Damascus? (9:11)
1. "Go to the house of Judas on Straight Street."
2. "Ask for a man from Tarsus named Saul."
3. *Both answers are correct.*

6. What happened when Ananias placed his hands on Saul? (9:17-18)
1. Saul's sight was restored and he ran away.
2. *Something like scales fell from Saul's eyes, and he could see again.*
3. Saul arrested Ananias and dragged him to prison.

7. What happened after Saul could see again? (9:18-19)
1. He was baptized.
2. He ate some food.
3. *Both answers are correct.*

8. When did Saul begin to preach in the synagogues in Damascus that Jesus is the Son of God? (9:20)
1. After about a week
2. After he received enough training
3. *At once*

9. Who baffled the Jews living in Damascus by proving that Jesus is the Christ? (9:22)
1. *Saul*
2. Ananias
3. Peter

10. Who took Saul to the apostles and told them about Saul? (9:27)
1. Peter
2. *Barnabas*
3. Ananias

Advanced competition

1. Against whom was Saul breathing out murderous threats? (9:1)
1. *The Lord's disciples*
2. The high priest
3. Only the twelve apostles
4. All of the answers are correct.

2. Why did Saul want letters for the synagogues in Damascus? (9:1-2)
1. So that he could tell them about the new high priest
2. *So that if he found anyone who belonged to the Way, he could put them in prison*
3. So he could tell them what they were doing wrong
4. So he would have permission to preach there.

3. What happened as Saul neared Damascus? (9:3-4)
1. Suddenly a light from heaven flashed around him.
2. He fell to the ground.
3. He heard a voice say to him, "Saul, Saul, why do you persecute me?"
4. *All of the answers are correct.*

4. The Lord said Saul was his chosen instrument. What would Saul do? (9:15)
1. He would lead the Jews into the promised land.
2. *He would carry the Lord's name before the Gentiles, their kings, and the people of Israel.*
3. He would persecute the Jews and the Gentiles.
4. He would punish anyone who stood in the way of the disciples.

5. Why did Saul's followers take him by night and lower him in a basket through an opening in the wall? (9:23-25)
1. Because the gates were locked
2. *Because the Jews conspired to kill him*
3. Because Saul's followers were ashamed of him
4. Because Saul was still blind

6. Who was afraid of Saul when he came to Jerusalem? (9:26)
1. The Jews and Gentiles
2. His friends and family
3. *The disciples*
4. Barnabas and John

7. What did Barnabas tell the apostles about Saul? (9:27)
1. How Saul on his journey to Damascus saw the Lord
2. How the Lord spoke to Saul
3. How in Damascus Saul preached fearlessly in the name of Jesus
4. *All of the answers are correct.*

8. What happened when the brothers learned that the Grecian Jews tried to kill Saul? (9:29-30)
1. *They took him down to Caesarea and sent him off to Tarsus.*
2. They arrested the Grecian Jews.
3. They guarded Saul with guns and spears.
4. They disowned Saul.

9. What happened to the church throughout Judea, Galilee, and Samaria? (9:31)
1. It enjoyed a time of peace.
2. It was strengthened.
3. It was encouraged by the Holy Spirit and grew in numbers.
4. *All of the answers are correct.*

10. Finish this verse: "Therefore if anyone is in Christ, he is a new creation; the old has gone, ..." (2 Corinthians 5:17)
1. "... to be forever forgotten!"
2. *"... the new has come!"*
3. "... and has been washed as white as snow!"
4. "... eternal life is yours!"

Acts 10:1-23

Basic Competition
To prepare the children for competition, read
Acts 10:1-23 to them.

**1. How does the book of Acts describe Cornelius
and his family? (10:2)**
1. *Devout and God-fearing*
2. Tax-collectors and sinners
3. Regular, normal people

2. Who appeared to Cornelius in his vision? (10:3)
1. The Lord
2. An indistinct figure
3. *An angel of God*

**3. About what time did Peter go up on the roof to
pray? (10:9)**
1. *At Noon*
2. At midnight
3. Both answers are correct.

**4. What did Peter see while he was praying?
(10:11-12)**
1. *He saw heaven opened and something like a
large sheet being let down to earth by its four
corners.*
2. He saw Cornelius's men approaching the city.
3. He saw an angel appear before him.

5. What did the large sheet contain? (10:12)
1. All kinds of four-footed animals
2. Reptiles of the earth and birds of the air
3. *Both answers are correct.*

**6. Peter said that he never ate anything impure or
unclean. What did the voice say afterwards?
(10:14-15)**
1. *"Do not call anything impure that God has made
clean."*
2. "You are correct, Peter, do not eat these
animals."
3. "The Lord has made these animals clean enough
to eat."

**7. How many times did Peter see the vision of the
large sheet? (10:16)**
1. One time
2. *Three times*
3. Ten times

**8. What did Peter ask the men that Cornelius sent?
(10:21)**
1. "What do you want to eat?"
2. *"Why have you come?"*
3. "Where will you stay the night?"

**9. Whom did Peter invite into the house to be his
guests? (10:19, 23)**
1. Cornelius
2. *The three men*
3. Both answers are correct.

**10. What did Peter do the day after his vision?
(10:23)**
1. *He went with Cornelius's men.*
2. He went to Jerusalem.
3. He went to the synagogue to pray.

Advanced Competition
**1. How does the book of Acts describe Cornelius?
(10:1-2)**
1. He was a devout and God-fearing man.
2. He gave generously to those in need.
3. He prayed to God regularly.
4. *All of the answers are correct.*

**2. How did Cornelius react to the angel of God?
(10:3-4)**
1. He fell to his knees.
2. *He stared at him in fear.*
3. He welcomed him into his house.
4. All of the answers are correct.

3. What happened while Peter prayed? (10:9-11)
1. He became hungry.
2. He fell into a trance.
3. He saw heaven opened and something like a
large sheet being let down to earth by its four
corners.
4. *All of the answers are correct.*

**4. What did a voice say to Peter when he saw the
sheet that contained different animals? (10:12-13)**
1. *"Get up, Peter. Kill and eat."*
2. "Share these animals with those who are
coming to see you."
3. "Sacrifice these animals at the temple."
4. "These animals are clean enough for you to eat."

5. What did Peter say that he had never eaten? (10:14)
1. Any animal of any kind
2. Any kind of fruit or vegetable
3. *Anything impure or unclean*
4. Anything with fat on it

6. What did the voice say after Peter said he never ate anything impure or unclean? (10:14-15)
1. *"Do not call anything impure that God has made clean."*
2. "You are correct, Peter, do not eat these animals."
3. "The Lord has made these animals clean enough to eat."
4. All of the answers are correct.

7. What did the Spirit say to Peter while he was still thinking about the vision? (10:19-20)
1. "Three men are looking for you."
2. "Get up and go downstairs."
3. "Do not hesitate to go with them, for I have sent them."
4. *All of the answers are correct.*

8. Who said, "I'm the one you're looking for. Why have you come?" (10:21)
1. Simon, the tanner
2. A man sent by Cornelius
3. *Peter*
4. Cornelius

9. Why did an angel tell Cornelius to ask Peter to come to Cornelius's house? (10:22)
1. *So that Cornelius could hear what Peter had to say*
2. So that Peter could prepare unclean animals for Cornelius
3. So that Cornelius could gain more respect from the Jewish people
4. All of the answers are correct.

10. The next day, who went with Peter and the three men? (10:23)
1. Simon the tanner and three men
2. *Some of the brothers from Joppa*
3. All of Peter's family
4. All of the answers are correct.

Acts 10:24 - 11:26
Basic Competition
To prepare the children for competition, read Acts 10:24-28, 34-48; 11:19-26 to them.

1. What did Cornelius do when Peter entered the house? (10:25)
1. He offered Peter something to eat.
2. *He fell at Peter's feet in reverence.*
3. He gave Peter a hug.

2. What did God show Peter? (10:28)
1. *That he should not call any man unclean or impure*
2. The directions to get to Cornelius's house
3. Everything he needed to know

3. Who does not show favoritism but accepts people from every nation who fear Him and do what is right? (10:34)
1. John
2. Paul
3. *God*

4. With what did God anoint Jesus? (10:38)
1. With oil and water
2. *With the Holy Spirit and power*
3. Both answers are correct

5. What happened to Cornelius, his relatives, and friends, while Peter was talking to them? (10:44)
1. Jesus appeared.
2. *The Holy Spirit came on them.*
3. Both answers are correct.

6. What did Peter hear when the gift of the Holy Spirit was given to the Gentiles at Cornelius's house? (10:46)
1. The sound of thunder
2. The voice of God
3. *The Gentiles speaking in tongues and praising God*

7. In whose name did Peter order that the Gentiles be baptized? (10:48)
1. *In the name of Jesus Christ*
2. In the name of the high priest
3. In the name of Cornelius

8. What did Barnabas encourage the people in Antioch to do? (11:23)
1. To turn from their wicked ways
2. *To remain true to the Lord with all their hearts*
3. To preach only to the Jews

9. Why did Barnabas go to Tarsus? (11:25)
1. To tell others the good news of Jesus Christ
2. To take a vacation
3. *To look for Saul*

10. What were the disciples called at Antioch? (11:26)
1. Followers
2. *Christians*
3. People of Jesus

Advanced competition

1. What happened when Peter entered Cornelius's house? (10:25-26)
1. Cornelius met Peter.
2. Cornelius fell at Peter's feet in reverence.
3. Peter said, "Stand up, I am only a man myself."
4. *All of the answers are correct.*

2. What did Peter tell Cornelius about Jesus and God? (10:40, 43)
1. God raised Jesus from the dead and caused him to be seen.
2. All the prophets testify about Jesus.
3. Everyone who believes in him receives forgiveness of sins through his name.
4. *All of the answers are correct.*

3. After Jesus was raised from the dead, who saw him? (10:41)
1. All the people
2. *Witnesses whom God chose*
3. All of the Jews
4. Only Jesus' family

4. What command did Jesus give to those who ate and drank with him after he rose from the dead? (10:41-42)
1. *To preach and to testify about him*
2. To heal and to cast out demons
3. To tear their clothes and to mourn
4. To celebrate and to dance

5. Who will receive forgiveness of sins through Jesus' name? (10:43)
1. Only the Jews
2. All the Gentiles
3. *Everyone who believes in Him*
4. Only those who ate and drank with him after he rose from the dead

6. What happened while Peter was speaking with Cornelius? (10:44)
1. The Jews got angry and left.
2. Heaven opened up and a dove landed on Peter's shoulder.
3. A large storm came and everyone got wet.
4. *The Holy Spirit came on all who heard the message.*

7. Why were the believers who had come with Peter astonished? (10:45-46)
1. *Because the gift of the Holy Spirit was poured out even on the Gentiles*
2. Because the Gentiles could not speak
3. Because the Gentiles were healed of all their diseases
4. All of the answers are correct.

8. How does the book of Acts describe Barnabas? (11:24)
1. An old man with a large family
2. *A good man, full of the Holy Spirit and faith*
3. A selfish and jealous man
4. All of the answers are correct.

9. What did Barnabas do when he found Saul in Tarsus? (11:25-26)
1. He told him everything he had seen and heard.
2. He begged to stay with him in Tarsus.
3. *He brought him to Antioch to meet with the church and teach.*
4. He sent him back to Jerusalem to preach to the Gentiles.

10. Where were the disciples first called Christians? (11:26)
1. Samaria
2. Tarsus
3. Jerusalem
4. *Antioch*

Acts 12:1-13:12

Basic Competition
To prepare the children for competition, read Acts 12:1-19; 13:1-12 to them.

1. Whom did King Herod have put to death with the sword? (12:2)
1. James, the brother of John
2. Barnabas
3. Peter

2. How did the church pray for Peter while he was in prison? (12:5)
1. Slowly
2. Earnestly
3. Once a week

3. Who suddenly appeared in the prison cell with Peter? (12:7)
1. An angel of the Lord
2. King Herod
3. The other Christians

4. What did Peter think was happening as he followed the angel out of the prison? (12:9)
1. He thought he was being kidnapped.
2. He thought it was his friend pretending to be an angel.
3. He thought he was seeing a vision.

5. What were many people doing at the house of Mary the mother of John? (12:12)
1. Worrying about Peter
2. Praying
3. Worshiping God

6. Who came to answer the door when Peter knocked at the outer entrance? (12:13)
1. Mary the mother of John
2. One of the apostles
3. A servant girl named Rhoda

7. How did the people feel when they opened the door and saw Peter? (12:16)
1. They were afraid.
2. They were astonished.
3. Both answers are correct.

8. Whom did the Holy Spirit say to set apart for him? (13:2)
1. Barnabas
2. Saul
3. Both answers are correct.

9. Who was Bar-Jesus? (13:6-7)
1. A Jewish sorcerer and false prophet
2. An attendant to Sergius Paulus
3. Both answers are correct.

10. What happened to Elymas the sorcerer when he opposed Barnabas and Saul? (13:6-11)
1. He became blind.
2. An angel struck him dead.
3. He was arrested.

Advanced Competition

1. What did King Herod do when he saw that James's death pleased the Jews? (12:2-3)
1. He killed James's brother, John, as well.
2. He put many others to death.
3. He seized Peter also.
4. Herod believed and was baptized.

2. How was Peter guarded in prison? (12:4)
1. By four squads of four soldiers each
2. By two soldiers outside the gate
3. By a full squadron of soldiers
4. By King Herod himself

3.What happened while Peter was sleeping between two soldiers, bound with two chains? (12:6-7)
1. Suddenly an angel of the Lord appeared.
2. A light shone in the cell.
3. The chains fell off Peter's wrists.
4. All of the answers are correct.

4. What happened first when the angel and Peter came to the iron gate leading to the city? (12:10)
1. It opened by itself.
2. The angel left Peter.
3. The guards caught Peter.
4. Peter realized that he was not dreaming.

5. Whom did the people at Mary's house think was at the door? (12:15)
1. Peter
2. An angel of the Lord
3. A guard looking for Peter
4. *Peter's angel*

6. What did Peter do when the people opened the door and saw him? (12:16-17)
1. He motioned with his hand for them to be quiet.
2. He described how the Lord had brought him out of prison.
3. He told them to tell James and the other brothers about his rescue.
4. *All of the answers are correct.*

7. What happened while the prophets and teachers in Antioch worshipped the Lord and fasted?(13:1-2)
1. They heard the news of Peter.
2. *The Holy Spirit said, "Set apart for me Barnabas and Saul."*
3. They were filled with pain at the death of James.
4. All of the answers are correct.

8. Who went down to Seleucia and sailed from there to Cyprus? (13:4)
1. *Barnabas and Saul*
2. Peter and John
3. The apostles
4. All of the prophets and teachers

9. What did Barnabas and Saul do when they arrived at Salamis? (13:5)
1. They preached to the Gentiles.
2. They baptized both Jews and Gentiles alike.
3. *They proclaimed the word of God in the Jewish synagogues.*
4. They healed people and cast out demons.

10. In what story does Saul's name change to Paul? (13:9)
1. The story about Stephen's stoning
2. The story about Saul's conversion
3. The story about Pentecost
4. *The story about Sergius Paulus and Bar-Jesus*

Acts 14:26 - 15:41

Basic Competition
To prepare the children for competition, read Acts 14:26-28; 15:1-12, 22-41 to them.

1. How long did Paul and Barnabas stay in Antioch with the disciples? (14:28)
1. For one month
2. For a few years
3. *For a long time*

2. Whom did the church send to Jerusalem to see the apostles and elders? (15:2-3)
1. *Paul and Barnabas*
2. The men from Judea
3. The Gentiles

3. How did the brothers feel when they heard the news of how the Gentiles had been converted? (15:3)
1. They were extremely upset.
2. *They were very glad.*
3. They were scared.

4. What did some believers who were also Pharisees say that the Gentiles must do? (15:5)
1. Be circumcised
2. Keep the Law of Moses
3. *Both answers are correct.*

5. How did God show that he accepted the Gentiles? (15:8)
1. By putting a mark on their heads.
2. By cursing the Jews' livestock.
3. *By giving the Holy Spirit to them*

6. Through what did Peter say we are saved? (15:11)
1. Through the Law of Moses and the prophets.
2. *Through the grace of our Lord Jesus*
3. Both answers are correct.

7. Who became silent as they listened to Barnabas and Paul telling about the miracles and wonders God did among the Gentiles? (15:12)
1. No one
2. *The whole assembly*
3. Only the apostles

8. The apostles and elders, with the whole church, decided to choose some of their own and send them to Antioch with Paul and Barnabas. Whom did they choose? (15:22)
1. *Judas and Silas*
2. Peter and John
3. Mary and Martha

9. What did Judas and Silas say in Antioch? (15:32)
1. They said very little.
2. *They said much to encourage and strengthen the brothers.*
3. They said exactly what the letter said.

10. What did Paul and Silas do in Syria and Cilicia? (15:40-41)
1. *They strengthened the churches*
2. They built new churches
3. Both answers are correct.

Advanced Competition

1. To whom did God open the door of faith? (14:26-27)
1. To the Jews
2. To Paul and Barnabas
3. *To the Gentiles*
4. To the apostles

2. Some men taught that one must be circumcised in order to be saved. Why did they believe this? (15:1)
1. *Because it was according to the custom taught by Moses*
2. Because it was according to the Gentile custom
3. Because it was according to the custom taught by Jesus
4. Because it was according to the custom in Antioch

3. Whose law did the Pharisees say that the Gentiles must be required to obey? (15:5)
1. The Law of the Gentiles
2. The Law of the Peter
3. *The Law of Moses*
4. The Law of the land

4. How did God show that he accepted the Gentiles? (15:8)
1. By setting them free from jail
2. By the power he gave to Peter
3. *By giving the Holy Spirit to them, just as he did to the Jews*
4. By sending them a vision

5. How did the letter to the Gentile believers in Antioch, Syria and Cilicia describe Barnabas and Paul? (15:26)
1. Men who were tired and in need of a place to rest
2. Men who would do anything for their fellow Jew
3. Men who needed to learn the Law of Moses
4. *Men who risked their lives for the name of our Lord Jesus Christ*

6. Why did the apostles and elders send Judas and Silas to Antioch? (15:27)
1. To see what was happening with the Gentiles
2. To ask them for money
3. *To confirm by word of mouth what they were writing*
4. To persecute the Gentiles

7. From what did the letter say the Gentiles should abstain? (15:29)
1. From food sacrificed to idols, and from blood
2. From the meat of strangled animals
3. From sexual immorality
4. *All of the answers are correct.*

8. Why did Paul not think that it was wise to take John, also called Mark, with them? (15:37-38)
1. Because he was a Gentile
2. Because he was ill and unfit for travel
3. Because he had a family that needed him
4. *Because he had deserted them in Pamphylia*

9. What happened because of Paul and Barnabas's sharp disagreement? (15:39)
1. They apologized and forgave each other.
2. *They parted company.*
3. They stopped preaching and teaching.
4. They took a vacation.

10. What did Paul do when he travelled through Syria and Cilicia? (15:41)
1. *He strengthened the churches.*
2. He decided to travel first by land and then by sea.
3. He asked Barnabas and Mark to join him.
4. All of the answers are correct.

Acts 16:6-40

Basic Competition
To prepare the children for competition, read Acts 16:6-40 to them.

1. Where did the Holy Spirit keep Paul and his companions from preaching the word? (16:6)
1. In Greece
2. *In Asia*
3. In Jerusalem

2. Why did Paul conclude that God called them to preach the gospel in Macedonia? (16:9-10)
1. *He had a vision of a man of Macedonia.*
2. He received a letter from Macedonia.
3. People urged him to go to Macedonia.

3. Whom did Paul and his companions find at the river on the Sabbath? (16:13-14)
1. Sadducees
2. *Lydia and some other women*
3. The brothers from Judea

4. How did the slave girl earn money? (16:16)
1. *By fortune-telling*
2. By selling fabrics and thread
3. By working as a cook

5. Why did the owners of the slave girl seize Paul and Silas? (16:19)
1. They wanted to make money off of their miracles.
2. *They realized that their hope of making money was gone.*
3. They were jealous of their powers.

6. What did Paul and Silas do at about midnight in prison? (16:25)
1. Pray
2. Sing hymns
3. *Both answers are correct.*

7. What caused the prison doors to fly open and everybody's chains to come loose? (16:26-27)
1. The prison guard decided to free everybody.
2. *A violent earthquake struck.*
3. There was an incredible thunderstorm.

8. The jailer asked Paul and Silas, "Sirs, what must I do to be saved?" What did they say? (16:31)
1. "You must let us go free."
2. "You must give a tithe to the synagogue."
3. *"Believe in the Lord Jesus, and you will be saved—you and your household."*

9. What did the jailer and his family do immediately? (16:33)
1. They freed Paul and Silas.
2. *They were baptized.*
3. They ran away.

10. Why was the jailer filled with joy? (16:34)
1. Because he was not punished for allowing Paul and Silas to escape.
2. Because he got off work early
3. *Because he had come to believe in God*

Advanced Competition

1. What happened when Paul and his companions tried to enter Bithynia? (16:7)
1. They passed easily through the border.
2. The border guards questioned them thoroughly.
3. *The Spirit of Jesus would not allow them to enter.*
4. They changed their minds and left.

2. Who said, "Come over to Macedonia and help us"? (16:9)
1. *A Macedonian man that Paul saw in a vision*
2. A Macedonian beggar on the road to Troas
3. The Macedonian government
4. The church in Macedonia

3. Who was Lydia? (16:14)
1. A dealer in purple cloth
2. A woman from Thyatira
3. A worshiper of God
4. *All of the answers are correct.*

4. In Philippi, a girl had a spirit by which she predicted the future. What happened after Paul became annoyed and said to the spirit, "In the name of Jesus Christ I command you to come out of her!" (16:18-20)
1. The spirit left the slave girl.
2. The owners of the slave girl seized Paul and Silas.
3. Paul and Silas were brought before the magistrates.
4. *All of the answers are correct.*

5. Why did Paul shout, "Do not harm yourself! We are all here!" (16:27-28)
1. To assure Silas that he was still there
2. *To prevent the jailer from killing himself because he thought the prisoners escaped.*
3. To stop the other prisoners from fighting each other.
4. Because the magistrate was about to beat the jailer for setting them free.

6. What did the jailer ask Paul and Silas? (16:29-30)
1. "How did this happen?"
2. "Are you magicians?"
3. *"What must I do to be saved?"*
4. "Where did you come from?"

7. Why was the jailer filled with joy? (16:34)
1. *Because he and his whole family came to believe in God*
2. Because the prisoners escaped
3. Because he was no longer the jailer
4. All of the answers are correct.

8. When did the magistrates send orders to release Paul and Silas? (16:35)
1. *At daylight*
2. That very night
3. A week later
4. After a fortnight

9. What did Paul want the magistrates to do? (16:37)
1. To quietly release them from prison.
2. *To come themselves and escort him and Silas out of prison.*
3. To publicly apologize for beating them.
4. All of the answers are correct.

10. Finish this verse: "Peter replied, 'Repent and be baptized, every one of you, in the name of Jesus Christ for the forgiveness of your sins. And you will receive ..." (Acts 2:38)
1. "... life everlasting."
2. *"... the gift of the Holy Spirit."*
3. "... riches of unknown measure."
4. "... everything the Lord has promised to you."

Acts 17:1-34

Basic Competition

To prepare the children for competition, read Acts 17:1-34 to them.

1. Who said, "This Jesus I am proclaiming to you is the Christ"? (17:1-3)
1. Silas
2. *Paul*
3. Timothy

2. In whose house did the Jews search for Paul and Silas? (17:5)
1. *Jason's house*
2. Mary's house
3. Lydia's house

3. What did the city officials do to Jason when they did not find Paul and Silas at his house? (17:6-9)
1. They flogged him.
2. They questioned him.
3. *They made him post bond.*

4. Who was sent to the coast when the Jews from Thessalonica went to Berea to stir up the crowds? (17:13-14)
1. *Paul*
2. Silas
3. Both answers are correct.

5. What distressed Paul while he was waiting for Silas and Timothy in Athens? (17:16)
1. It was taking them a long time to get there.
2. He could not speak their language.
3. *The city was full of idols.*

6. What was inscribed on an altar in Athens? (17:23)
1. "To the Lord Jesus Christ"
2. *"To an unknown god"*
3. "To the people of Athens"

7. What does God give all men? (17:25)
1. *Life and breath and everything else*
2. All of the riches of the world
3. Anything we ask for

8. Who is not far from each one of us? (17:27)
1. Paul
2. *God*
3. Peter

9. What did some of the Athenians' poets say? (17:28)
1. We belong to him.
2. We are heirs to the kingdom.
3. *We are his offspring.*

10. How did God prove that he has set a day when he will judge the world with justice? (17:31)
1. *By raising Jesus from the dead*
2. By giving Paul the words to say
3. By offering judgment on earth

Advanced Competition

1. In Thessalonica, what did the Jews do because they were jealous? (17:5)
1. They repented and were baptized.
2. They beat up Paul and Silas.
3. *They formed a mob and started a riot in the city.*
4. They sent their high priest to prison.

2. Of what did the Jews in Thessalonica accuse Paul and Silas? (17:6-7)
1. *Of defying Caesar's decrees, saying that there is another king*
2. Of harboring enemies among them
3. Of visiting the homes of sinners
4. Of performing miracles on the Sabbath

3. How did the Bereans receive the message? (17:11)
1. Reluctantly
2. Slowly, after consulting their priests
3. With closed minds
4. *With great eagerness*

4. What did the Jews in Thessalonica do when they learned that Paul was preaching the word of God at Berea? (17:13)
1. They left Berea.
2. *They agitated the crowds in Berea.*
3. They calmed the crowds in Berea.
4. All of the answers are correct.

5. Paul debated a group of philosophers. What remark did some of them make? (17:18)
1. "He is trying to stir up trouble."
2. *"He seems to be advocating foreign gods."*
3. "This man preaches the truth."
4. "He is simply teaching."

6. What did all the Athenians and the foreigners who lived there spend their time doing? (17:21)
1. *Talking about and listening to the latest ideas*
2. Whatever they pleased
3. Worshipping their idols
4. Entertaining guests

7. How did Paul know that the men of Athens were very religious? (17:22-23)
1. *He found an altar with this inscription: "To an Unknown God."*
2. They had pictures of Jesus on the walls.
3. They obeyed the Law and the Prophets.
4. He found proof that Jesus was there.

8. While in Athens, how does Paul describe God? (17:24)
1. As a jealous God
2. As a God who is unattainable
3. *As the Lord of heaven and earth*
4. As an angry God

9. Who gives all people life, breath, and everything else? (17:24-25)
1. Paul
2. *God*
3. Zeus
4. Athena

10. For what has God set a day? (17:31)
1. "When he will flood the whole earth"
2. *"When he will judge the world with justice"*
3. "When he will prove his power"
4. "When he will return"

Acts 18:1-11, 18-28

Basic Competition
To prepare the children for competition, read
Acts 18:1-11, 18-28 to them.

1. Where did Paul go after he left Athens? (18:1)
1. To Thessalonica
2. *To Corinth*
3. To Antioch

2. Why did Paul stay with Aquila and Priscilla? (18:2-3)
1. *Because he was a tentmaker like them*
2. Because they had a lot of money
3. Because they were from Italy

3. In Corinth, what did Paul do every Sabbath? (18:4)
1. *He reasoned in the synagogue.*
2. He worked as a tentmaker.
3. He went home to Tarsus.

4. Who told Paul, "Do not be afraid; keep on speaking, do not be silent"? (18:9)
1. *The Lord, in a vision*
2. Barnabas and Timothy
3. The believers in Corinth

5. How long did Paul stay in Corinth? (18:11)
1. For two weeks
2. *For a year and a half*
3. Not very long

6. Why did Paul have his hair cut off at Cenchrea? (18:18)
1. Because his hair was too long
2. Because he did not want anyone to recognize him
3. *Because of a vow he had taken*

7. What did Paul do throughout the region of Galatia and Phrygia? (18:23)
1. *Strengthened all the disciples*
2. Hid among the Gentiles
3. Both answers are correct.

8. What was the only baptism Apollos knew about? (18:25)
1. The baptism of Peter
2. *The baptism of John*
3. The baptism of Jesus

9. What did Priscilla and Aquila do for Apollos? (18:26)
1. Invited him to their home
2. Explained to him the way of God more adequately
3. *Both answers are correct.*

10. What did Apollos do upon arriving in Achaia? (18:27-28)
1. He vigorously refuted the Jews in public debate.
2. He proved from the Scriptures that Jesus was the Christ.
3. *Both answers are correct.*

Advanced Competition
1. Why did Aquila and Priscilla come from Italy to Corinth? (18:1-2)
1. Because they had friends and family there
2. *Because Claudius had ordered all the Jews to leave Rome*
3. Because they were looking for work in Corinth
4. Because Priscilla needed a vacation

2. What did Paul do in the synagogue every Sabbath? (18:4)
1. *He reasoned and tried to persuade Jews and Greeks.*
2. He preached when the rabbi was not there.
3. He told of his travels.
4. He condemned the sinners.

3. What did Paul say when the Jews opposed him and became abusive? (18:6)
1. "Your blood be on your own heads!"
2. "I am clear of my responsibility."
3. "From now on I will go to the Gentiles."
4. *All of the answers are correct.*

4. Who accompanied Paul to Syria? (18:18)
1. Barnabas and Timothy
2. *Priscilla and Aquila*
3. The brothers
4. No one

5. In Ephesus, what did Paul do when the Jews asked him to spend more time with them? (18:19-21)
1. He accepted.
2. *He declined, but promised to come back if it was God's will.*
3. He told them that he would pray about it.
4. He decided to stay for two more weeks.

6. How does the book of Acts describe Apollos? (18:24-25)
1. He was a learned man, with a thorough knowledge of the Scriptures.
2. He had been instructed in the way of the Lord, and he spoke with great fervor and taught about Jesus accurately.
3. He knew only the baptism of John.
4. *All of the answers are correct.*

7. What did Priscilla and Aquila do when they heard Apollos? (18:26)
1. *They explained to him the way of God more adequately.*
2. They condemned him.
3. They sent word to Paul asking him to return immediately.
4. They quietly asked him to leave.

8. In Achaia, who was a great help to those who by grace had believed? (18:27)
1. Paul
2. Barnabas
3. *Apollos*
4. All of the answers are correct.

9. In Achaia, what did Apollos prove from the Scriptures? (18:28)
1. That Paul was the Christ
2. That the creation story was true
3. *That Jesus was the Christ*
4. That God judges everyone

10. According to Romans 8:31, who is for us? (Romans 8:31)
1. No one
2. All of the believers
3. *God*
4. The Lord Jesus Christ

Acts 19:1 - 20:12

Basic Competition

To prepare the children for competition, read Acts 19:1-12, 23-41; 20:7-12 to them.

1. How many men were baptized and received the Holy Spirit in Ephesus? (19:5-7)
1. Hundreds
2. *About twelve*
3. Just a few

2. What happened after the disciples in Ephesus were baptized and Paul placed his hands on them? (19:5-6)
1. The Holy Spirit came on them.
2. They spoke in tongues and prophesied.
3. *Both answers are correct.*

3. Who did extraordinary miracles in Ephesus? (19:11)
1. The disciples
2. *God, through Paul*
3. Everyone who believed

4. About what did there arise a great disturbance in Ephesus? (19:23)
1. *About the Way*
2. About Paul's past
3. About which man-made god was the greatest

5. Who was Demetrius? (19:24)
1. A preacher in Ephesus
2. *A silversmith who made shrines to the goddess Artemis*
3. A sorcerer

6. What did Paul say that man-made gods are? (19:26)
1. Foolish
2. Beautiful statues
3. *No gods at all*

7. After Paul said that man-made gods were not gods, what happened? (19:26-29)
1. *The whole city of Ephesus was in an uproar.*
2. Those worshiping in the shrines of Artemis were happy.
3. The disciples were upset.

8. In the theatre in Ephesus, whom did the Jews push to the front? (19:33)
1. Paul
2. *Alexander*
3. Demetrius

9. What did the city clerk in Ephesus say that Paul and his men did not do? (19:37)
1. They did not rob the temples.
2. They did not blaspheme their goddess.
3. *Both answers are correct.*

10. What happened to Eutychus when he fell asleep in the window? (20:9-10)
1. He fell to the ground and died.
2. Paul put his arms around him and told everyone that he was alive.
3. *Both answers are correct.*

Advance Competition

1. What did Paul ask the disciples upon arriving in Ephesus? (19:1-2)
1. "Has Apollos been here?"
2. "How many Christians are there here?"
3. *"Did you receive the Holy Spirit when you believed?"*
4. "Do you remember who I am?"

2. Why did Paul leave some of the people in Ephesus? (19:9)
1. They became obstinate.
2. They refused to believe.
3. They publicly maligned the Way.
4. *All of the answers are correct.*

3. What happened when the handkerchiefs and aprons that touched Paul were taken to the sick? (19:12)
1. The sick got worse and passed away.
2. *Their illnesses were cured and the evil spirits left them.*
3. The handkerchiefs and aprons magically disappeared.
4. The Holy Spirit came upon the sick.

4. How does the book of Acts describe Demetrius? (19:24)
1. He was a silversmith.
2. He made shrines of Artemis.
3. He brought in no little business for the craftsmen.
4. *All of the answers are correct.*

5. What did Demetrius say would lose its good name? (19:27)
1. *The silversmith trade*
2. The Lord, Jesus Christ
3. The worshippers of Artemis
4. All of the answers are correct.

6. What did the workmen shout when they heard what Demetrius said? (19:28)
1. "Long live the King!"
2. "We believe in Jesus Christ!"
3. *"Great is Artemis of the Ephesians!"*
4. "Arrest Paul and persecute him!"

7. Of what is the city of Ephesus the guardian? (19:35)
1. Of many gods and goddesses
2. *Of the temple of Artemis and of her image*
3. Of the written word of God
4. All of the answers are correct.

8. What did the city clerk say Demetrius and his fellow craftsmen could do? (19:38)
1. Remain if they were peaceful
2. Riot in the streets as long as they wanted to
3. *Press charges if they had a grievance against anybody*
4. Make idols of different gods

9. What happened to Eutychus while Paul was preaching? (20:9-10)
1. He fell asleep.
2. He fell out of the window.
3. He died.
4. *All of the answers are correct.*

10. What did Paul do after he raised Eutychus from the dead? (20:10-11)
1. He stopped preaching and went home.
2. *He broke bread, ate, and talked until daylight.*
3. He told Eutychus to stay awake.
4. All of the answers are correct.

Acts 20:17- 21:19

Basic Competition
To prepare the children for competition, read Acts 20:17-24, 32-38; 21:17-19 to them.

1. How did Paul teach in Ephesus? (20:20)
1. Publicly
2. From house to house
3. *Both answers are correct.*

2. What did Paul declare to both Jews and Greeks? (20:21)
1. That they must turn to God
2. That they must have faith in Jesus
3. *Both answers are correct.*

3. Who compelled Paul to go to Jerusalem? (20:22)
1. *The Spirit*
2. An angel
3. Barnabas

4. What did Paul consider that his life was worth? (20:24)
1. Everything
2. *Nothing*
3. Only a little

5. What did the Holy Spirit warn Paul of in every city? (20:23)
1. That prison was facing him
2. That hardships were facing him
3. *Both answers are correct.*

6. What did Paul not covet? (20:33)
1. Silver or gold
2. Clothing
3. *Both answers are correct.*

7. According to the words of the Lord Jesus, "It is more blessed to give than to..." (20:35)
1. "...take from others."
2. *"...receive."*
3. "...have too much."

8. What grieved the elders in Ephesus the most? (20:38)
1. *Paul saying that they would never see his face again*
2. That Paul was coming back soon
3. That they could not go with Paul

9. What did the brothers do when Paul and his companions arrived at Jerusalem? (21:17)
1. *They received them warmly.*
2. They arrested them.
3. They gave them medical attention.

10. About what did Paul tell James and the elders when he arrived in Jerusalem? (21:19)
1. About the problems that the Jews caused
2. *About what God did among the Gentiles*
3. Both answers are correct.

Advanced Competition

1. How did Paul serve the Lord while he lived in Ephesus? (20:17-19)
1. With fear and trembling
2. *With great humility and with tears*
3. With confidence and strength
4. With uncertainty and insecurity

2. How did Paul teach in Ephesus? (20:20)
1. With hesitation
2. *Publicly and from house to house*
3. While standing on a platform
4. Only to a small group of believers

3. What did Paul declare to both Jews and Greeks in Ephesus? (20:21)
1. That the gods of Ephesus were false gods
2. Everything that he knew
3. *That they must turn to God in repentance and have faith in the Lord Jesus*
4. Only what they could handle

4. Where did the Holy Spirit warn Paul that prison and hardships were facing him? (20:23)
1. In Jerusalem
2. In Asia
3. *In every city*
4. In the Jewish synagogues

5. To what did Paul commit the elders of the church? (20:32)
1. To each other
2. *To God and to the word of his grace*
3. To the leading of Silas and Timothy
4. To the people of Ephesus

6. Whose hands supplied Paul's needs? (20:34)
1. His companions' hands
2. The disciples' hands
3. The Gentiles' hands
4. His own hands

7. What happened after Paul finished speaking to the Ephesian elders? (20:36-37)
1. He knelt down and prayed.
2. They all wept.
3. They embraced him and kissed him.
4. All of the answers are correct.

8. Who received Paul and the others warmly when they arrived at Jerusalem? (21:17)
1. The brothers and sisters
2. No one
3. Everyone they saw
4. Only the twelve apostles

9. About what did Paul report, in detail, when he arrived in Jerusalem? (21:19)
1. About how the people of Ephesus did not believe
2. About the riots he had seen
3. About what God did among the Gentiles through his ministry
4. All of the answers are correct.

10. Finish this verse: "However, I consider my life worth nothing to me, if only I may finish the race and complete the task the Lord Jesus has given me..." (Acts 20:24)
1. "...and win the gold medal."
2. "...the task of testifying to the gospel of God's grace."
3. "...even though the task is very hard."
4. "...and live a life of eternity in heaven."

Acts 21:27 - 22:29

Basic Competition
To prepare the children for competition, read Acts 21:27—22:3, 17-29 to them.

1. Whom did the Jews assume Paul brought into the temple area? (21:29)
1. Peter
2. Cornelius
3. Trophimus

2. What happened immediately after the Jews dragged Paul from the Temple? (21:30)
1. They killed Paul.
2. Paul regained strength.
3. The gates were shut.

3. In Jerusalem, what did the rioters do when they saw the commander and his soldiers? (21:32)
1. They scattered.
2. They stopped beating Paul.
3. Both answers are correct.

4. In Jerusalem, who arrested Paul and ordered him to be bound with two chains? (21:33)
1. The commander
2. The rioters
3. The Jerusalem officials

5. Why did the soldiers carry Paul up the steps to the barracks? (21:35)
1. Because Paul could not walk.
2. Because James tried to prevent Paul from leaving.
3. Because the crowd was too violent.

6. In what language did Paul speak to the crowd in Jerusalem? (21:40)
1. Aramaic
2. Greek
3. Latin

7. What did the crowd do when they heard Paul speak in Aramaic? (22:2)
1. They rioted.
2. They became very quiet.
3. They immediately believed in Jesus Christ.

8. Where did the Lord say he would send Paul? (22:21)
1. To the people of Jerusalem
2. To an unknown location
3. Far away to the Gentiles

9. What did Paul say when the commander asked if he was a Roman citizen? (22:27-28)
1. "Yes, I am. I was born a citizen."
2. "No, I was just teasing."
3. "I am a citizen of the Kingdom of God."

10. Finish this verse: "Now go; I will help you speak and will..." (Exodus 4:12)
1. "...protect you from all harm."
2. "...reward you greatly."
3. *"...teach you what to say."*

Advanced Competition

1. What happened while the rioters were trying to kill Paul? (21:31)
1. The Greeks took over the temple.
2. *News reached the commander of the Roman troops.*
3. Paul was taken into heaven.
4. All of the Jews were seized.

2. What did the commander order? (21:33)
1. *He ordered that Paul be bound with two chains.*
2. He ordered his soldiers to execute Paul.
3. He ordered that Paul receive a fair trial.
4. He ordered his soldiers to defend themselves.

3. Why did the commander order that Paul be taken into the barracks? (21:34)
1. Because Paul was defiant
2. Because the crowd loved him and wanted him to stay in their town.
3. *Because he could not get at the truth because of the uproar*
4. All of the answers are correct.

4. Who did the commander think Paul was? (21:38)
1. A false prophet
2. An escaped prisoner
3. A very dangerous person
4. *An Egyptian who started a revolt*

5. What happened when the crowd heard Paul speak to them in Aramaic? (22:2)
1. *They became very quiet.*
2. They were outraged.
3. The Holy Spirit came upon them all.
4. The commander stopped him from speaking.

6. What happened to Paul when he was praying in the Temple in Jerusalem? (22:17-21)
1. Paul fell into a trance.
2. The Lord told Paul to leave Jerusalem because the people would not accept his testimony about him.
3. The Lord said that he was sending Paul to the Gentiles.
4. *All of the answers are correct.*

7. What did Paul do when the blood of Stephen was shed? (22:20)
1. He attempted to stop those who were killing him.
2. He turned his face so that he did not have to watch.
3. *He stood there giving his approval.*
4. He did nothing.

8. What did Paul ask if it was legal to do? (22:25)
1. *To flog a Roman citizen who has not been found guilty*
2. To arrest someone without proof of their offense
3. To kill him without notifying his family
4. To flog anyone without a fair trial

9. What was Paul's answer when the commander asked, "Are you a Roman citizen?" (Acts 22:27)
1. "No, I am not."
2. "I was born a Roman citizen, but I am no longer."
3. *"Yes, I am."*
4. "I will not tell you."

10. In Jerusalem, why was the commander alarmed? (22:29)
1. Because Paul got sick in prison
2. Because Paul escaped from prison
3. Because he did not know what to do with Paul
4. *Because he put a Roman citizen in chains*

Acts 22:30—23:35

Basic Competition
To prepare the children for competition, read Acts 22:30—23:24, 31-35 to them.

1. What did Ananias, the high priest, order those standing near Paul to do? (23:2)
1. Whip Paul on the back
2. *Strike Paul on the mouth*
3. Kill Paul

2. What did Paul say after he insulted the high priest? (23:4-5)
1. "I did not realize that he was the high priest."
2. "For it is written: 'Do not speak evil about the ruler of your people.'"
3. *Both answers are correct.*

3. What happened after Paul said that he stood on trial because of his hope in the resurrection of the dead? (23:6-7)
1. Paul was released.
2. *A dispute broke out between the Pharisees and the Sadducees.*
3. Paul was sentenced to life in prison.

4. What was the commander afraid would happen to Paul because the dispute became so violent in the Sanhedrin? (23:10)
1. *Paul would be torn to pieces by them.*
2. Paul would escape into the crowd.
3. Both answers are correct.

5. While in Jerusalem who stood near Paul and encouraged him? (23:11)
1. The commander
2. The disciples
3. *The Lord*

6. Who formed a conspiracy and bound themselves with an oath not to eat or drink until they killed Paul? (23:12)
1. The disciples
2. *Some Jews in Jerusalem*
3. Both answers are correct.

7. When did the Jews plan to kill Paul in Jerusalem? (23:15)
1. When he was put in prison
2. *While he was on the way to the Sanhedrin*
3. When Paul was on a ship to Rome

8. Who overheard the plot to kill Paul? (23:16)
1. Paul's sister
2. Paul's brother-in-law
3. *The son of Paul's sister*

9. Why did the commander order a detachment of 200 soldiers, 70 horsemen, and 200 spearmen to go to Caesarea? (23:23-24)
1. To fight the Jews
2. *To escort Paul safely to Governor Felix*
3. To assist the Jews in killing Paul

10. Where was Paul to be kept in Caesarea? (23:35)
1. In the prison
2. *In Herod's palace*
3. Both answers are correct.

Advanced Competition

1. After he arrested Paul, what did the commander do the next day? (22:30)
1. He wanted to find out exactly why Paul was being accused by the Jews.
2. He released Paul.
3. He ordered the chief priests and the Sanhedrin to assemble.
4. *All of the answers are correct.*

2. What did Paul call Ananias, the high priest? (23:3)
1. An evil man
2. *A whitewashed wall*
3. A godly man
4. A gracious person

3. What did Paul say the high priest, Ananias, did by commanding that he be struck? (23:3)
1. Committed a great sin
2. Hurt his feelings
3. *Violated the law*
4. All of the answers are correct.

4. Why did a dispute break out between the Pharisees and the Sadducees? (23:7-8)
1. The Sadducees say that there is no resurrection.
2. The Sadducees say that there are neither angels nor spirits.
3. The Pharisees acknowledge the resurrection, angels, and spirits.
4. *All of the answers are correct.*

5. In a vision, while in Jerusalem, where did the Lord say that Paul would go to testify? (23:11)
1. *To Rome*
2. To Samaria
3. To Judea
4. To Asia

6. What were more than forty men involved in? (23:12-13)
1. A conspiracy
2. An oath not to eat or drink
3. A plot to kill Paul
4. *All of the answers are correct.*

7. What did the son of Paul's sister do when he heard about the plot to kill Paul? (23:16)
1. He kept it a secret.
2. He formed an army to fight the Jews.
3. *He went into the barracks and told Paul.*
4. He prayed for God's protection.

8. Whom did the commander order to go to Caesarea at nine o'clock on the night he learned of the plot? (23:23)
1. 200 soldiers
2. 70 horsemen
3. 200 spearmen
4. *All of the answers are correct.*

9. Where was Paul to be kept under guard in Caesarea? (23:35)
1. In the home of the governor
2. In prison
3. *In Herod's palace*
4. On the streets

10. According to 2 Corinthians 1:10b, what did Paul say that God would continue to do? (2 Corinthians 1:10b)
1. God will continue to call apostles to serve him.
2. God will serve us.
3. *God will continue to deliver us.*
4. God will find us when we need him the most.

Acts 25:23—26:32

Basic Competition

To prepare the children for competition, read Acts 25:23—26:32 to them.

1. Who came with great pomp and entered the audience room? (25:23)
1. Agrippa
2. Bernice
3. *Both answers are correct.*

2. Why did Festus bring Paul before Agrippa? (25:26)
1. Festus was angry at Paul and wanted someone else to punish him.
2. *Festus wanted to know what to write about Paul in the letter to Caesar.*
3. Festus wanted Agrippa to have faith in Jesus.

3. Why did Paul consider himself fortunate to stand before King Agrippa? (26:2-3)
1. Because Agrippa was not a Jew
2. *Because Agrippa was acquainted with the Jewish customs*
3. Because Agrippa was rich and powerful

4. What did Paul beg King Agrippa to do? (26:3)
1. To set him free
2. To punish the Jews
3. *To listen patiently to him*

5. Whom did Paul say that he put in prison in Jerusalem? (26:10)
1. Those who did not pay taxes
2. *Many of the saints*
3. The governor of Jerusalem

6. Where was Paul going when a light from heaven blazed around him? (26:12-13)
1. Jerusalem
2. Emmaus
3. *Damascus*

7. To whom would Christ bring the message of light? (26:23)
1. To His own people
2. To the Gentiles
3. *Both answers are correct.*

8. Who said that Paul was out of his mind? (26:24)
1. Agrippa
2. *Festus*
3. Bernice

9. What did Paul say about himself during his speech to Festus? (26:25)
1. "I am not insane, most excellent Festus."
2. "What I am saying is true and reasonable."
3. *Both answers are correct.*

10. With what was King Agrippa familiar? (26:25-26)
1. With all the laws of Moses
2. *With the things that Paul was saying*
3. Both answers are correct.

Advanced Competition

1. How did Agrippa and Bernice enter the audience room? (25:23)
1. They entered with great pomp.
2. They entered with the high-ranking officers.
3. They entered with the leading men of the city.
4. *All of the answers are correct.*

2. Why did Festus decide to send Paul to Rome? (25:25)
1. Because Paul deserved to be executed
2. *Because Paul made his appeal to the Emperor*
3. Because Felix told him to send him there
4. Because Paul offended Festus

3. Who gave Paul permission to speak for himself? (26:1)
1. Festus
2. The commander
3. *Agrippa*
4. All of the answers are correct.

4. Why did Paul say that he was on trial? (26:6)
1. Because the Jews hated him
2. *Because of his hope in what God had promised their fathers*
3. Because he preached to the Gentiles
4. Because Festus could not decide Paul's fate

5. What did Paul see on the road to Damascus? (26:13)
1. An angel of the Lord
2. Nothing
3. One crippled beggar
4. *A light from heaven*

6. What did Paul do before he saw Jesus on the road to Damascus? (26:9-10)
1. *He did all that was possible to oppose the name of Jesus.*
2. He supported the church in all they did.
3. He worked as a tax collector.
4. He raised his children.

7. What message did Paul preach in Damascus, Jerusalem, and all Judea? (26:19-20)
1. That they should repent
2. That they should turn to God
3. That they should prove their repentance by their deeds
4. *All of the answers are correct.*

8. What did Festus say was driving Paul insane? (26:24)
1. *His great learning*
2. His unbelievable teachings
3. His prison sentence
4. His unshakable faith

9. What did Agrippa say to Festus? (26:32)
1. *"This man could have been set free if he had not appealed to Caesar."*
2. "He should not have preached to the Gentiles."
3. "He broke the law and should be punished."
4. "He is surely an angel and not a man."

10. What did Peter and John say when they were told not to speak or teach at all in the name of Jesus? (Acts 4:20)
1. *"We cannot help speaking about what we have seen and heard."*
2. "You should not judge others."
3. "Do not threaten us!"
4. All of the answers are correct.

Acts 27:1-44

Basic Competition

1. When did Paul's ship begin sailing? (27:9)
1. After Pentecost
2. *After the Fast*
3. In December

2. Who warned that the voyage would be disastrous and bring great loss? (27:9-11)
1. Julius
2. The pilot and the owner of the ship
3. *Paul*

3. What swept down from the island? (27:14)
1. A wind of hurricane force
2. A "northeaster"
3. *Both answers are correct.*

4. What did the sailors do for fear that they would run aground on the sandbars of Syrtis? (27:17)
1. They lowered the sea anchor
2. They let the ship be driven along
3. *Both answers are correct.*

5. What did the sailors throw overboard on the third day? (27:19)
1. The slaves
2. *The ship's tackle*
3. The food

6. What did Paul urge the men to do after they lost hope of being saved? (27:22)
1. *To keep up their courage*
2. To turn around and sail home
3. To send out a call for help

7. During his voyage on the ship, in what did Paul have faith? (27:25)
1. That everyone on board would die, except him
2. That the islanders would attack them
3. *That everything would happen just as God told him*

8. After they ate as much as they wanted, how did the sailors lighten the ship? (27:38)
1. *By throwing the grain into the sea*
2. By throwing the prisoners overboard
3. By cutting loose the anchors

9. Whose life did the centurion want to spare? (27:43)
1. All of the sailors' lives
2. His own life
3. *Paul's life*

10. Who reached land in safety? (27:44)
1. Only the soldiers
2. Only the prisoners
3. *Everyone*

Advanced Competition
1. Who was Julius? (27:1)
1. The soldier that escorted Paul and some other prisoners to Rome
2. A centurion
3. A member of the Imperial Regiment
4. *All of the answers are correct.*

2. Whose advice did the centurion follow? (27:11)
1. *The advice of the pilot and the owner of the ship*
2. The advice of the centurion's wife
3. The advice of Paul
4. His own advice

3. What was the wind of hurricane force called? (27:14)
1. A typhoon
2. *The northeaster*
3. A bolt of lightning
4. The Great Storm

4. What did the sailors do with the boat when it was caught in a storm? (27:17-19)
1. They passed ropes under the ship to hold it together.
2. They lowered the sea anchor and let the ship be driven along.
3. They threw the cargo and tackle overboard.
4. *All of the answers are correct.*

5. What did the angel of God tell Paul on the ship? (27:23-24)
1. Do not be afraid.
2. You must stand trial before Caesar.
3. God has graciously given you the lives of all who sail with you.
4. *All of the answers are correct.*

6. On the ship, what did Paul do with the bread? (27:35)
1. *He gave thanks to God, broke it, and ate it.*
2. He threw it overboard.
3. He was not hungry.
4. All of the answers are correct.

7. What happened when they hoisted the foresail to the wind and made for the beach? (27:40-41)
1. The ship struck a sandbar and ran aground.
2. The bow stuck fast and would not move.
3. The stern was broken to pieces by the pounding of the surf.
4. *All of the answers are correct.*

8. Who kept the soldiers from carrying out their plan to kill the prisoners on board? (27:43)
1. Paul
2. The owner of the ship
3. The island people
4. *The centurion*

9. What order did the centurion give to some of the prisoners? (27:43-44)
1. *He ordered those who could swim to jump in and swim to land.*
2. He ordered those who could not swim to tie themselves to the mast of the ship.
3. He ordered a few of the prisoners to escape in the lifeboats.
4. All of the answers are correct.

10. Finish this verse: "Let us hold unswervingly to the hope we profess,..." (Hebrews 10:23)
1. "...for life is short."
2. "...for you cannot put your hope in people."
3. *"...for he who promised is faithful."*
4. "...for you never know what may happen tomorrow."

Acts 28:1-31

Basic Competition

To prepare the children for competition, read Acts 28:1-31 to them.

1. What happened when Paul put a pile of brushwood on the fire? (28:3-5)
1. A snake bit Paul on the hand.
2. Paul shook the snake off into the fire.
3. *Both answers are correct.*

2. Who welcomed Paul and his companions to his home and entertained them for three days on the island of Malta? (28:7)
1. The king of Malta
2. *The chief official of the island, Publius*
3. Several of the widows of Malta

3. Who came to Paul after he healed Publius's father? (28:9)
1. *The rest of the sick on the island*
2. All of Publius's family
3. The chief officials of Malta

4. What did the islanders of Malta do for Paul and the crew? (28:10)
1. Honored them in many ways
2. Furnished them with the supplies that they needed
3. *Both answers are correct.*

5. What happened when Paul saw the brothers from Rome? (28:15)
1. *He thanked God and was encouraged.*
2. He was angry at them because they put him in prison.
3. He asked them why they did not come see him in Jerusalem.

6. Why did the leaders of the Jews in Rome want to hear Paul's views? (28:22)
1. *Because people everywhere were talking against this sect*
2. Because they were excited to hear Paul's testimony
3. Because they received a letter from Jerusalem concerning Paul

7. When did the Jewish leaders in Rome begin to leave Paul? (28:25)
1. *After Paul made his final statement*
2. Around noon
3. Immediately after Paul began teaching about Jesus Christ

8. What did Paul say was sent to the Gentiles? (28:28)
1. Dreams and visions
2. *God's salvation*
3. Pain and suffering

9. What did Paul say that the Gentiles would do with the message of God's salvation? (28:28)
1. They would toss it aside.
2. They would not listen to it.
3. *They would listen to it.*

10. How long did Paul stay in Rome? (28:30)
1. *Two years*
2. Two months
3. Two weeks

Advanced Competition

1. What did the islanders of Malta do for Paul and his companions? (28:1-3)
1. Showed unusual kindness
2. Built a fire for them
3. Welcomed them
4. *All of the answers are correct.*

2. Why did the islanders say that Paul was a murderer? (28:4)
1. Because Paul was performing miracles
2. Because Paul seemed guilty and nervous
3. *Because Paul was bitten by a snake*
4. All of the answers are correct.

3. What happened to Paul when the snake bit him? (28:5-6)
1. *Paul suffered no ill effects.*
2. Paul swelled up.
3. Paul suddenly fell dead.
4. Paul became like God.

4. How was Publius's father healed? (28:8)
1. Paul went to see him.
2. Paul prayed for him.
3. Paul placed his hands on him and healed him.
4. *All of the answers are correct.*

5. What did Paul do when he saw the brothers in Rome? (28:14-15)
1. *He thanked God and was encouraged.*
2. He hugged them and cried.
3. He turned his face from them because he was ashamed.
4. He asked for food and a place to stay.

6. Why did Paul say that he was bound with a chain? (28:20)
1. Because he committed a crime deserving death
2. *Because of the hope of Israel*
3. Because his own people were guilty
4. All of the answers are correct.

7. How did Paul try to convince those in Rome about Jesus? (28:23)
1. Through miraculous signs
2. *From the Law of Moses and from the Prophets*
3. Through stories of his travels
4. By telling them that he loved them

8. What did Paul say was sent to the Gentiles? (28:28)
1. Money to build new churches
2. *God's salvation*
3. Pain and suffering
4. Persecution

9. What did Paul say that the Gentiles would do with the message of God's salvation? (28:28)
1. They would toss it aside.
2. They would not listen to it.
3. *They would listen to it.*
4. They would not know what it means.

10. What did Paul do for two years while in Rome? (28:30-31)
1. He stayed in his own rented house.
2. Boldly and without hindrance, he preached the kingdom of God.
3. He taught about the Lord Jesus Christ.
4. *All of the answers are correct.*

Children's Quizzing Score Sheet

Instructions: Basic Quizzing uses only questions 1-15. Advanced quizzing uses 20 questions. Read the rules and stick to them.

Names: Round 1	1	2	3	4	5	6	7	8	9	10	11	12	13	14	15	16	17	18	19	20	Total
Team Bonus																					

Team Total

Names: Round 1	1	2	3	4	5	6	7	8	9	10	11	12	13	14	15	16	17	18	19	20	Total
Team Bonus																					

Team Total

Names: Round 1	1	2	3	4	5	6	7	8	9	10	11	12	13	14	15	16	17	18	19	20	Total
Team Bonus																					

Team Total